On Sovereignty and Other Political Delusions

THEORY FOR A GLOBAL AGE

Series Editor: Gurminder K. Bhambra, University of Warwick, UK.

Editorial Board: Michael Burawoy (University of California Berkeley, USA), Neera Chandoke, (University of Delhi, India) Robin Cohen (University of Oxford, UK), Peo Hansen (Linköping University, Sweden) John Holmwood (University of Nottingham, UK), Walter Mignolo (Duke University, USA), Emma Porio (Ateneo de Manila University, Philippines), Boaventura de Sousa Santos (University of Coimbra, Portugal).

Globalization is widely viewed as the current condition of the world, only recently come into being. There is little engagement with its long histories and how these histories continue to have an impact on current social, political, and economic configurations and understandings. Theory for a Global Age takes 'the global' as the already-always existing condition of the world and one that should have informed analysis in the past as well as informing analysis for the present and future. The series is not about globalization as such, but, rather, it addresses the impact a properly critical reflection on 'the global' might have on disciplines and different fields within the social sciences and humanities. It asks how we might understand our present and future differently if we start from a critical examination of the idea of the global as a political and interpretive device; and what consequences this would have for reconstructing our understandings of the past, including our disciplinary pasts.

Each book in the series focuses on a particular theoretical issue or topic of empirical controversy and debate, addressing theory in a more comprehensive and interconnected manner in the process. With books commissioned from scholars from across the globe, the series explores understandings of the global – and global understandings – from diverse viewpoints. The series will be available in print, in eBook format and free online, through a Creative Commons licence, aiming to encourage academic engagement on a broad geographical scale and to further the reach of the debates and dialogues that the series develops.

Also in the series:	Forthcoming titles:
Connected Sociologies Gurminder K. Bhambra	*The Black Pacific: Anticolonial Struggles and Oceanic Connections* Robbie Shilliam
Eurafrica: The Untold History of European Integration and Colonialism Peo Hansen and Stefan Jonsson	*John Dewey: The Global Public and its Problems* John Narayan
Postcolonial Piracy: Media Distribution and Cultural Production in the Global South Edited by Lars Eckstein and Anja Schwarz	*Stark Utopia: Debt as a Technology of Power* Richard Robbins and Tim Di Muzio
	Cosmopolitanism and Antisemitism Robert Fine and Philip Spencer
	Debating Civilizations: Interrogating Civilizational Analysis in a Global Age Jeremy Smith

On Sovereignty and Other Political Delusions

Joan Cocks

B L O O M S B U R Y

LONDON • NEW DELHI • NEW YORK • SYDNEY

Bloomsbury Academic

An imprint of Bloomsbury Publishing Plc

50 Bedford Square	1385 Broadway
London	New York
WC1B 3DP	NY 10018
UK	USA

www.bloomsbury.com

Bloomsbury is a registered trade mark of Bloomsbury Publishing Plc

First published 2014

© Joan Cocks, 2014

No responsibility for loss caused to any individual or organization acting on or refraining from action as a result of the material in this publication can be accepted by Bloomsbury Academic or the authors.

British Library Cataloguing-in-Publication Data
A catalogue record for this book is available from the British Library.

ISBN: HB: 978-1-7809-3353-5
PB: 978-1-7809-3354-2
ePub: 978-1-7809-3355-9
ePDF: 978-1-7809-3356-6

Library of Congress Cataloging-in-Publication Data
A catalog record for this book is available from the Library of Congress.

Typeset by Fakenham Prepress Solutions, Fakenham, Norfolk NR21 8NN

Contents

Series Editor's Foreword

In this important book, *On Sovereignty and Other Political Delusions*, Joan Cocks unsettles conventional concepts within Western political theory; in particular, that of sovereignty, and related notions of sovereign power and sovereign freedom. While such concepts are often considered in territorially bounded terms, she re-imagines them from the perspective of an inter-related world. In addition, the standard accounts treat specific 'polities' and 'peoples', usually those of the Westphalian settlement, as exemplary. Instead, with her elegant prose and humanist commitments, Cocks highlights the political experiences of people who have not been central to the making of political theory. She does this by examining the confrontations between European settlers and indigenous peoples in the lands that were to become the United States of America and also by analysing the precipitating factors and subsequent effects of the Jewish search for sovereign freedom in Palestine. According to Cocks, these two cases demonstrate the complex ways in which both the ideas and practices of sovereign freedom and domination are mutually imbricated.

On Sovereignty and Other Political Delusions clearly demonstrates the necessity of rethinking our social and political concepts and paradigms from a perspective that acknowledges the connectedness of the worlds within which we live. This is one of the key aims of the Theory for a Global Age series and one that Cocks fulfils admirably. She both challenges the standard historical narratives that underpin these profoundly important concepts and calls on us to question the disciplinary practices that have enabled such partial accounts to stand for so long. Indeed, her book presses us to renovate key political concepts, not only because of their increasing incongruity with new substantive conditions of globalization, but also as a critical response to the price that already has been paid during the historical course of their translation from theory to practice.

This is a powerfully argued book that is open to existing historiography and political sensitivities while nonetheless forging a clear path through the complexities that often serve to obscure more than enlighten. It is an exemplary piece of scholarship that deserves the widest audience and deep engagement.

Gurminder K. Bhambra

Acknowledgments

My deepest thanks to Kavita Datla, Karuna Mantena, and Elizabeth Markovits for their perceptive comments at a workshop on an early draft of this manuscript and for their ebullient company that afternoon. Much thanks, as always, to Peter Cocks, who served as both a perpetual sounding board and a dedicated if stringent critic, and to Karen Remmler, who was delicately attuned to the inner spirit of this book. I owe a debt to Gurminder Bhambra, who—not for the first time—prodded me to contribute to a project she was spearheading. Caroline Wintersgill put up with my endless emails from America and remained a pleasure to work with throughout the entire process; the imaginative and patient cover designer, Paul Burgess, must hope never again to deal with an author who cares about how shadows fall on the image of a rock. Kim Storry was a painstaking project manager. Thanks to the Mellon Foundation for funding our comparative empire faculty seminar at Mount Holyoke College. My appreciation also goes to Amy Martin and Richard Payne for their thoughts on the logical relationship of empires to nation-states and their responses to a paper that became the backbone of Chapter 2 of this book; to Yves Winter, for organizing our Johan Galtung-on-violence panel at an American Political Science Association annual convention a number of years ago; and to Uday Mehta and Amrita Basu, for asking me to join their Five-College seminar on political violence, and for being, with the other members, such stimulating conversationalists. Thanks to Falguni Sheth and Bonnie Honig for recommending this project for college funding and for our intellectual interchanges in the past, as well as to Sayres Rudy, Jim Scott, Dustin Howes, and Ron Shaw for useful bibliographical tips. Last but not least, I'd like to recognize all the students at Mount Holyoke College who accepted my invitation to tackle, in successive semesters over the last decade, the meaning of sovereign power, political violence, citizenship, exile, and nationalism.

While they came from places as far apart as Serbia, Pakistan, South Korea, Egypt, China, Albania, India, the Occupied Territories, Nepal, and different corners of the United States, these undergraduates avidly pursued the same vexing intellectual and political questions when they found themselves sharing a seminar table in a small liberal arts college in Western Massachusetts. I dedicate this book to them.

A section of Chapter 2 originally appeared in my article, "Foundational Violence and the Politics of Erasure," in "Violence: Systemic, Symbolic, and Foundational," ed. Brandon Absher, Anatole Anton, and José Jorge Mendoza, special issue, *Radical Philosophy Review* 15, no. 1 (2012): 103–26.

Several passages in Chapter 3 originally appeared in my article, "Jewish Nationalism and the Question of Palestine," in "Edward W. Said and Questions of Nationalism," ed. Gurminder K. Bhambra, special issue, *Interventions: International Journal of Postcolonial Studies* 8, no. 1 (2006): 24–39.

Where possible, I've included, in brackets in the endnotes and in parentheses in the bibliography of this book, the original date of publication of each cited author's work when it differs significantly from the date of publication of the edition from which I am citing.

Introduction

A maelstrom is shattering the world's partly separated pasts, sweeping all of its regions into a jarring present, and threatening to hurtle the privileged, the ordinary, and the wretched of the earth towards a future that is ecologically and politically distressed. This maelstrom often goes by the name of "globalization" or is referred to in terms of one or other of globalization's aspects, such as climate change, the digital revolution, identity fracture, the age of terror, the total surveillance society, global empire. Walter Benjamin once alluded to the shocks of modernity through his now-famous image of an angel of history who looks backwards at wreckage piled upon wreckage while being catapulted forwards by the storm "we call progress."[1] Three-quarters of a century later, the shocks have been so ratcheted up that the term "post-modern" was coined to convey our fraught situation. In one way, however, we face the same dilemma that Hannah Arendt described in her biographical sketch of Benjamin and much of the rest of her work. Concepts, values, and ideals that for so long had seemed reliable and attractive have become inadequate or irrelevant. Yet, those habits of thought are all we have to begin to grasp our predicament—or rather, predicaments, since there are many different hurricanes in our great storm, and many different degrees of insulation from their impact at least in the short run.

The political ideas the world has inherited, whether willingly or not, from the Western tradition are deeply implicated in the current breakdown in the relationship between conventional thought and the new realities that human practice is bringing into being. A few concepts, such as "direct democracy" or "the industrial proletariat," soon may be so out of synch with those realities, dovetailing with conditions that no longer prevail, that except as historical descriptors or metaphors they might as well be permanently shelved.[2] Many others, such as "citizenship" or "security," need to be radically overhauled. Some concepts, such as "privacy" or "the commons," point to experiential losses that we can try to recover in a modified form once we are aware that they *are* losses, identifying half-buried but appealing and still distantly viable alternatives to the range of possibilities we see now. That range might be widened by exposing the Western tradition to inherited ideas from the rest of the world—as, for example, the possibilities for pluralism might be widened by the Ottoman idea of the millet system. Finally, some concepts will turn out to have helped precipitate many of our current crises in the first place, even as those crises are now undermining the allusive power of those concepts. In these last cases, a conceptual loss that at first glance is unthinkable and at second glance is regrettable may in fact be an opening to a more promising way of imagining and acting in the world. It will be the argument of this meditation, which mostly looks backwards to prepare for a different way of imagining forwards, that "sovereignty" is one such promising loss.

While we differ over whether the idea of sovereignty deserves the treatment he more generally prescribes, my efforts dovetail with James Tully's call for political theory to become "a critical activity" that "starts from the practices and problems of political life, but … begins by questioning whether the inherited languages of description and reflection are adequate to the task." Political theory, as Tully sees it, should seek not only to understand the "repertoire of problems and solutions in question, and the correlative field of relations of power in contestation" but also to release the grip of restricting "patterns of thought and reflection" and horizons of practice that have "come to be experienced as necessary rather than contingent, constitutive rather than regulative, universal rather than partial."[3] A release of thought and practice from the dream of sovereign power is the hope that animates this book.

Although, as we shall see later, the concept is highly complex, sovereignty can be summed up here as the power to command and control everything inside a physical space. The conventional associations of the term oscillate, as William E. Connolly notes, between "acting with final authority" and "acting with irresistible power,"[4] but the term also connotes exclusivity in the sense of acting over against or as opposed to another, for without an actual, potential, or imagined competitor, no assertion of sovereignty would ever have to be made. The core argument I advance about such assertions is two-pronged. First, sovereign power is an end that it is possible to strive for but impossible to arrive at, and never more impossible than now. Second, the struggle to gain freedom through sovereign power is not only more delusional but also potentially more dangerous than the attempt to attain sovereign power *per se*. It will take the rest of these pages to probe the delusional aspects of sovereign freedom, but its dangers can be hinted at here. Classical monarchical sovereign power even in its idealized form was frank about the need for domination, although its sometimes partial and sometimes absolute refusal of political agency to underlings was touted as serving not only the majesty of the monarch but also the needs of its subjects for order, security, and the continued enjoyment of whatever liberties were accorded to them. Modern popular sovereign power sought to free itself from dominating higher authorities to determine the conditions of life for itself. However, by cutting potential bonds of identification with those outside the sovereign body and elevating a particular people and its mode of life above those marked as alien, it opened new possibilities for domination both inside and outside the territorial boundaries of the sovereign state.

Many democratic theorists have focused on the domestic organization of sovereign power, typically at the level of the modern nation-state. They have argued with one another over the extent to which authoritative power in democratic nation-states is monolithic or pluralist, resides in a system of laws or a people with its own disruptive tendencies and alternative traditions, is concentrated in a single executive or "monarch" or shared among various governmental institutions, social groups, individual citizens, and ebullient if ephemeral multitudes. While these arguments have influenced my thinking, my meditations more centrally concern the relationship between even the most democratically organized sovereign states and the life worlds that had to be vanquished for them to *become* sovereign. The target of my critique is not political societies on the scale of the large territorial modern state but the sovereign conceit and ambition of modern states large or small, as well as the same conceit and ambition on the part of the individual, the ethnos, the demos, and the human race as a single entity.

Although it has earlier variants, the idea of *sovereign freedom* examined here is quintessentially modern, along with the idea of the sovereign individual, ethnonational sovereignty, popular sovereignty, and the dream that the human race might rule the earth and eventually even the universe.[5] Yet the realists among my readers might wonder whether the will to *sovereign power* is historically specific or instead is rooted in what is conventionally called human nature. My intuition, which is realist in a different way, is that such a will is a highly mediated form of an elemental desire of human beings to survive and thrive in an environment not initially made *by* them, but waiting *for* them. So—a response to the world outside the self, worked up into a socially and historically contingent impulse to obliterate, expel, or rule other inhabitants of that world instead of being at their mercy, but also instead of reveling in them for what they are, merging with them, mixing with them as equals, or simply letting them be.

Chapter 1 examines the contested character of political concepts in general and the concept of sovereignty in particular, as well as other keywords with which the idea of sovereign power has been entangled. The next two chapters are a pair of case studies of the interplay of freedom and domination in attempts to attain sovereign power, to display both its seductions and its oppressive effects. Chapter 2 probes the American Indian Treaty System to illustrate the violent foundations of sovereign power even in the instance of republican or liberal democratic sovereign states, and even when "peaceable" deliberation, negotiation, consent, and rule by law are key mechanisms of those states' birth and the expansion of their authority. Chapter 3 probes the struggle for Jewish sovereignty to solve the problem of the minority status of a diasporic group in the age of the modern nation-state, which, in its consequences for both Israeli Jews and Palestinian Arabs, illustrates the delusion of sovereign freedom. Between them, these twin cases cover civic national and ethnonational avenues to popular sovereign statehood, casting a shadow on the endeavors of either building a house where, as Arendt would put it, freedom can live or building a safe house from ethnic persecution.

While some might object that the dominative elements in the American founding and the Jewish search for sovereign freedom can be traced to their being settler colonial projects, it would take very little effort to export the critique of sovereign freedom from settler to non-settler contexts. Another way to put the point is that even on "home territories," attempts to gain freedom through sovereign power via, for example, ethnonational movements, political partitions, revolutionary regime changes, or modern state-building also are settler projects of a sort, as each of these new political orders must "settle" the society it "colonizes," by [re-]establishing the territorial boundaries within which it is to be authoritative, [re-]wiring laws within those bounds, [re-]configuring identities and habits of life for the people it declares to be "its" people, and determining who will be counted as that people's new enemies. Thus settler states in the literal sense of that term, rather than being exceptions to the rule, can be seen as extreme exemplars of sovereign power entrenchment. Their foreignness to the societies they penetrate is more exaggerated than the foreignness of partitions, revolutions, and modernizations that radically disrupt and remake societies from within. The refusal of settler colonists to identify with the people whose lives they are steamrolling over is more absolute, and the experience of those at the receiving end of that refusal is consequently more devastating, humiliating, and abject. Nevertheless, the drive to conquer and supplant already existing modes of existence, and the disregard for those attached to that existence, characterize colonial settlers, ethnonationalists, secessionists, revolutionaries, and modernizers alike.

The decision to highlight the cases of the American founding and Jewish nationalism flows partly from the fact that these two cases helped convince me that sovereign freedom and domination are inextricably intertwined. But that decision also is rooted in my belief that political theory must take its substantive problems from and ground its conclusions in actual political affairs instead of floating about those affairs in a heavenly realm of pure thought, where categories may interact with one another in captivating ways without having any relation to the ends that are pursued in the political world, the means used to pursue them, and the passions of those who, in addition to using means to pursue ends, react often viscerally, impulsively, or self-subversively to circumstances and events. Here I strongly endorse Karuna Mantena's critique of neo-Kantian political theory and her call for "another realism" that begins "from an understanding of the existing conditions and constraints of political life" but "neither forsakes an agenda of reform nor sacrifices ethics at the altar of power politics."[6] However, in contrast with Mantena, who emphasizes the political primacy of means over ends and endorses means that are non-violent, my two cases illustrate problems with specific political ends that become apparent when one studies their practical implications, and that are problematic regardless of whether or not direct violence is used to pursue them.

Given that political theory's expertise is in concepts, principles, ideas, and norms, the political theorist who looks backwards in time to assess political ideals in light of what happens when political actors try to actualize them almost inevitably will find herself leaning on the work of professional historians. This political theorist is greatly indebted to the meticulous research of the many historians drawn on here. Nonetheless, the difficulties I encountered while trespassing on the historian's terrain should be acknowledged up front. With respect to the American case, the eradication of indigenous life worlds that paved the way for the birth and continental expansion of the United States was absent from many of the stories told by the American founding's most admiring chroniclers, an absence that the very phrase "the American founding" emblemizes. But the more daunting problems are the obstacles to discovering how indigenous peoples of North America understood the world before the arrival of

European settlers, and, more specifically, whether there had been a conceptual analogue of "sovereignty" in pre-Columbian indigenous languages, or whether the counter-sovereignty struggles of native Americans were struggles for something introduced as a good by their European antagonists. Answers to these questions are typically filtered through European settler perspectives in the past that either dismissed the value of pre-Columbian perspectives altogether or read back into them settler presumptions about how the world is conceptually divided up. Alternatively, those answers are filtered through indigenous perspectives in the present that have long since been transformed by the indigenous–settler encounter and that in any event clash on the cultural origins of the sovereignty concept.

The case of Zionism presents its own problems of inaccessibility, if only because some of the writings of the Zionists I examine have yet to be translated into English or are translated in widely varying ways. But multiplying the hazards of this case study one hundredfold is the fact that the history of Zionism is so vituperatively contested. To read Zionist and Palestinian accounts of that history is like peering through a telescope at two planets at opposite ends of the universe. Beyond the almost total discrepancy between "pro-Israel" and "pro-Palestinian" interpretations of the struggle for a Jewish state, and between those who locate the original impetus of Zionism in settler colonialism and those who locate it in the struggle for national liberation, there are large discrepancies between left- and right-wing Zionist versions of that struggle, between the claims of adulatory and revisionist Israeli historians, and between Zionist, post-Zionist, and anti-Zionist postures toward the same past. This hornets' nest of warring perspectives is only aggravated by the shifting political positions and self-interpretations on the part of Zionists at different stages of their lives, and, at any given stage, by incongruities in what they say to different audiences. Especially Theodor Herzl and Vladimir Jabotinsky, who were writing and speaking not to muse but to persuade, knew full well that one does not say the same thing, in the same tone, to the Ottoman Sultan, members of the British Parliament, skeptical Jewish philanthropists, and young Palestinian (as Jewish settlers were called before 1948) pioneers. Finally, in the case of Jabotinsky, one is also dealing with an esthete who for that reason would be judged by strict empiricists as an unreliable narrator. Even political theorists who do not believe that "pure facts" can be precipitated out from all rhetorical forms in which facts are articulated must tread carefully while reading lines from this Zionist's riveting pen. For, as he declares in the conclusion of his micro-historical memoir, *The Story of the Jewish Legion*, Jabotinsky sees truth as in important ways a function of beauty.

> Without any bias, I have omitted a number of facts; for I do not believe that every fact is true in the fundamental sense. A great thing has a character—"features"; whatever is expressive of those features is part of the truth; whatever is in contradiction of that character is an accident, a scar, a rash … when one wishes to relate the essence of an episode, the beauty of which must today be universally affirmed, it is puerile to examine the mud—even though mud gathers where people gather … The memory is an autonomous mechanism, and a petty one. It attracts tiny details, especially unpleasant ones, and does not like to detach itself from them. That is why we have been vouchsafed a controlling apparatus which we call "taste."[7]

One other, different point is worth making about political theory's interpretation of the tie between the present and the past. I concur with Hannah Arendt that human beings are capable of breaking with ossified practices or pernicious patterns of social life to begin something new, sometimes something astoundingly new. I also concur with what I take to be Patchen Markell's insistence that "beginning something new" takes place in response to an established context, itself the outcome of actions taken by others in the past against the backdrop of their own established contexts. That is, the "miracle of action" does not signify total rupture with the past or a human capacity to wipe clean the slate of history to start afresh, however assiduously some people may try to do that, but rather a new orientation of the self with respect to an always already given world.[8] Still, it would be an error to underestimate the forces arrayed against even context-bound reorientations. One of the patterns this book explores is the tendency of those oppressed by sovereign power to make counter-sovereignty bids to save themselves. While any whiff of inevitability that the reader might sense in the case studies should not be taken as signaling the inescapable role of sovereign power in human affairs, it does reflect a dynamic by which, once power is organized along sovereign lines, collective movements for freedom are propelled to reach their goal by mobilizing the resources of sovereign power for themselves. Strategic thinking is not the only compelling factor here. Resentment of the privileges of sovereignty incites desires to possess as readily as it incites desires to dispel those privileges, and perhaps more readily. If breaking with the self-replicating logic of sovereign power and the investments in sovereign freedom it triggers is the kind of miracle of action for which Arendt would and did hope, calculation and sentiment conspire to ensure that this particular miracle will not be easy to pull off.

After pursuing intimations of non-sovereign freedom in the contemporary Israeli–Palestinian conflict, my Conclusion extrapolates a critical-analytical, a political, and an ecological lesson from both case studies. While these lessons are hardly original, they have yet to be memorized by the relevant "us."

The critical-analytical lesson flows from the fact that the erasures that typify sovereign political foundings also typify capitalism as it re-settles the globe to suit its imperatives (and, indeed, political and economic processes of erasure often have gone hand in hand). It follows that critics of capitalism should attend to the obliteration of non-capitalist identities and practices no less avidly than they do to the new identities and practices that capitalism generates. This is not only because obliteration is capital's "first" (if often-repeated) violent act; it is also because sensibilities buried by capital may be worth reactivating once they are unearthed.

The political lesson is that, to reduce the tribulations while enhancing the agency of people around the world who have become "wandering Jews," our century must find ways to de-link the right of individuals to participate in the making of common arrangements from membership in a people with exclusive power in and control over a specific territory. The ecological lesson is that, for the sake of all the life species, including our own, a concern for place and a love of what I will call "natural freedom" must supplant the self-defeating quest to make human beings sovereign masters of the planet.

Two notes on what I am *not* arguing in this book. While I will be emphasizing the link between sovereign freedom and domination, my point is not to woo readers to the side of established sovereign powers against people struggling for sovereign freedom from those powers. To the contrary, my point is to extend a sympathetic warning to the strugglers that they are likely to re-create for others the political injuries they are trying to escape for themselves unless they find a way to transcend the sovereign power ideal. And, while some may detect a pessimistic slant to my musings, it is not because I think that every feature of the past is preferable to the present or that all hope for the future is now lost. With respect to human–human relations, I mean to be warily upbeat, not only because even in its darkest hours history has pleasantly surprised us before (although it has unpleasantly surprised us, too), but also because promising new varieties of thought and action always can be found in the cracks and crevices of any political status quo. With respect to human–earth relations, however, the prospects are a great deal grimmer because of the global expansion of an unsustainable mode of production, consumption, and culture. I hope to show that the quest for sovereign freedom is one element in an admittedly far more complex array of forces pushing the earthly home of living things to the edge of its precipice.

As the next chapter should prime us to expect, every argument about political concepts, to the extent that it enters into the general discourse, is likely to provoke further intellectual debate and political controversy. Attacks on the concept of sovereign freedom are no exception to this rule. But this is the destiny of all political ideas—to be perpetually provocative, until the day that some inconceivable metamorphosis in the human condition, perhaps the unintended result of human action, makes them irrelevant for good.

1

The Sovereignty Concept

Concepts and politics

The terms of political discourse are the words we use to talk about problems and possibilities in the political world, but they also are problems and possibilities in themselves. "Power," "justice," "equality," "tyranny," and so on are, first of all, intellectual puzzles without definitive solutions, in that any conceptualization of any of these terms will spark its own revision, refinement, extension, or counter-conceptualization when it inevitably is found to be inadequate to its object in some way. In turn, those contrasting concepts will spark new chains of revisions, refinements, and counter-concepts. Magnifying the undecidability of each political keyword is the fact that its conceptualization involves the use of other keywords (sometimes political, but sometimes philosophical, aesthetic, religious, or economic) that are intellectual puzzles without definitive solutions, too.

Take, for example, the classical liberal definition of freedom proposed by J. S. Mill in *On Liberty*. The individual is free to the extent that he can form his own thought and feeling, opinions and sentiments, tastes, associations, goals for action, and style of life. The only justifiable limits to this "sovereignty of the individual over himself" are that he must not harm other individuals and must share in the "labors and sacrifices incurred for defending the society or its members from injury and molestation."[1] In short, the free individual can pursue his self-regarding interests without interference by others but is obligated to contribute to their collective security and refrain from injuring them. While at first glance Mill's proposition seems straightforward, it has provoked in many inquiring minds, simply because they *are* inquiring minds, a host of new questions about freedom and the other key terms on which Mill relies. What constitutes injury to another? Are any interests purely self-regarding? What is a self? Are sovereignty and freedom synonyms?

Every term of political discourse is not just an intellectual but also a political Pandora's box. People with clashing ideological commitments in the world also will clash over the meaning of the keywords they use to talk about the world and even may go to war because, to stay with our example, they value freedom but disagree in part about what freedom means and who is its proper subject. Thus, in a case in which one society tries to export the requisite institutions and habits of thought and practice to support freedom in some twenty-first-century revision of the Millian sense of that term, and another society denies that the individual self is sovereign, sees freedom's most significant subject as the collective culture, and defines freedom as national self-determination, not just conceptual debate but also political conflict may ensue. It is a weird and unfortunate fact of political life that if conflict does ensue, the relative material power of the two sides rather than the relative intellectual worth of their competing concepts will determine which idea of freedom is victorious.[2]

In a classic gem of an essay, W. B. Gallie characterizes aesthetic, religious, and political discourse as pivoting on concepts over which disputes are likely to erupt without the possibility of an "objective" or universally agreed-upon resolution. Concepts are essentially contestable if they are intellectually open ended, in the sense we noted above of being susceptible to further elaborations and revisions; internally complex, containing many ideational aspects; and inherently appraisive, in describing a phenomenon with an intrinsic value that can be over-ridden only by strong reasons pertaining to special circumstances, whether that value is positive (as according to Gallie's original formulation) or negative (once other scholars had expanded it).[3] In *The Terms of Political Discourse* William E. Connolly explains how essential contests over political concepts occur and why those contests are themselves political.[4] Those who use the same political keyword may not agree on an entire list of its internal aspects, although they will agree on enough of those aspects to feel that their disagreements are about the same general idea. They may agree on the list of aspects but rank the importance of each differently. They may clash over the conceptualization of other keywords on which the definition of this one relies. They may place this value on different rungs of a hierarchy of all shared or partly shared positive values. Thus, our Millian individualist and champion of national–cultural self-determination both see freedom as a good and autonomy as a central internal aspect of the concept, while disagreeing about the sanctity of individual self-regarding interests, what a self is (self-authoring and atomistic or indelibly stamped by its membership in a larger social whole), and whether the value of freedom should be ranked higher than, lower than, or on the same level as the values of solidarity and cultural integrity. Because they have an overlapping sense of what "freedom" means and because they are both invested in it as a good, it will be impossible to resolve their conflict by giving the term "freedom" to one party's concept and coining a new term for the other's.

What also will be impossible is for scholars of politics to evade or resolve or transcend the essentially contested nature of political keywords in their own analyses of politics. The conceit of positivistic social science to stand outside the world it seeks to explain hinges on its ability to develop a vocabulary that is substantively uncontroversial, normatively neutral, with universally agreeable rules for the construction and application of terms. However, if scholars of politics wish to clarify and illuminate the world of politics, they at some point will have to draw on the everyday language of politics to describe that world, which means that they will have to use essentially contested concepts of politics in specific ways, defining "democracy," for example, in the liberal democratic instead of right- or left-populist sense when they describe certain political societies as "democratic." In doing so, whether intentionally or unwittingly, they ally themselves with actors who endorse that definition against others who do not. Hence, in addition to whatever political positions they may have in their capacity as members of the political world that inform or seep into their work, scholars of politics will be pulled by the logic of essentially contested concepts into the world as they analyze it, instead of being able to dissect it from a god's eye point of view. If those scholars instead try to assume a scientific stance by devising a new language—say, a mathematical one—from which all internally complex, inherently appraisive, and open-ended concepts have been excised, their statements may achieve a veneer of value-neutrality, objectivity, and universalizability, but what they have to say with those statements will clarify little about the world as it is inhabited and understood by political actors and hence be of interest mostly to political scientists as a specialized professional group. I say "veneer," because the superiority of value-neutrality for gaining insight into human affairs is itself a value position, pitted against, for example, a recognition of the inevitability of having a stake in those affairs and the superiority of having a stake that is self-conscious and self-reflective.

Political keywords are problems and possibilities in themselves not only because they are intellectually open-ended and politically contested but also because they are historical phenomena. Their internal aspects, associations, and even evaluative thrust undergo metamorphoses over time, both in response to and in anticipation of changes in practical circumstances. This is the point to which Raymond Williams is attuned in *Marxism and Literature* when he tracks the changes in the English word "culture" from its early connotation of the cultivation of crops to its later connotation of self-cultivation and learning, along with its competing connotation of a whole way of life. Magnifying this historical flexibility is the fact that the terms from which "culture" is distinguished change over time as well, although not always at the same pace or for the same reasons. Thus, as Williams recounts, "society" conjured up the idea of shared fellowship when "culture" conjured up crop cultivation but later came to signify that which is abstract, mechanical, industrial, and economic, over against which culture came to signify literature, the arts, meaning, values, and inner, subjective experience.[5]

Past inflections of keywords often remain sedimented in the present connotations of those same words. That the past leaves its traces on categories in the present means that the words we use in political life may, by evoking elements of a world that is disappearing or already has largely disappeared, prevent us from identifying and grasping the new lineaments of our own world. The capacity of everyday terms to attach the imagination to ossified forms of thought tied to evaporating forms of practice was one of Antonio Gramsci's worries about the effect of inherited ideas on a peasantry subordinated to landowning elites and the Catholic Church as Italy moved towards an industrial capitalist future. Although with a different political agenda, Michel Foucault flags the same antiquated potentiality of language when he declares that a preoccupation with "sovereignty" on the part of scholars of politics is a hangover from the age of monarchical rule that blinds them to new micro-modalities of modern power.

As Williams notes, however, residues of the past in our current terminology also can provide us with tools for identifying, criticizing, and staunching the human losses that those new lineaments entail. To cite a current example, the English keyword "the commons" once connoted forests, meadows, and fields available for use by everyone until that land was enclosed by rural aristocrats, gentry, and other improving farmers for private profit-making. Today, because of its residual references, "the commons" has become an evocative keyword for critics of the neo-liberal project of privatizing or "enclosing" all public or collective goods.[6]

Then again, as Williams also is right to note, the triumph in the present of some historical meaning of a term over other, partially discrepant meanings it had had in the past can blind us to possibilities of practice conjured up by those defeated meanings. Quentin Skinner, who agrees with Williams here, praises the intellectual historian for acting "as a kind of archaeologist, bringing buried intellectual treasure back to the surface, dusting it down and enabling us to reconsider what we think of it."[7] Skinner cites, as an example, the contemporary hegemony of the classical liberal notion of liberty as a sphere of action not blocked by external impediments. The notion of liberty as non-interference, which conceivably could be secured for the individual by autocratic political rule, conflicts with and helps obscure an older, neo-roman notion of liberty as non-dependence on the will, even the goodwill, of a superior power. The actualization of *this* idea of liberty invites a quest for the self-governance of citizens as the necessary condition of non-dependence. It is a contention of this book that once-experienced features of "self-rule" (in the not necessarily individualistic sense of "self") were obscured once the idea of self-rule was swept under the sovereignty rubric.

The missed opportunities of defeated meanings aside, the historicity of political keywords gives our imagination, speech, and action a density of meaning of which any individual speaker and actor may or may not be aware, as the participants in the general assemblies of Occupy Wall Street benefited but may or may not have recognized the descent of their thought and practice from the French Revolution and the political theory of Jean-Jacques Rousseau. What happens to this enriching historical density of language in the event of drastic breaks in historical continuity? In the mid-twentieth century, Hannah Arendt believed that the rise of totalitarianism reduced all inherited Western political concepts to shards and fragments, forcing its survivors to dig through the rubble for conceptual insights that might be salvaged for use in a radically new but not thereby improved world. Today, many intellectuals wonder whether globalization represents another kind of concept-shattering historical break.

To see just how shattering this break might be, we need to make one last point about political concepts: they are formed not just in time but also in space. At least until now, political concepts always have emerged in and have responded to life in particular places, even if they sometimes purport to pertain to all places. The local derivation and reference of political ideas hardly means that they remain rooted in one spot. They can travel spontaneously, as Edward Said put it, from one place to another on the wings of speech and the written word, their connotations mutating as they go. Alternatively, these terms can be imposed by a stronger society in one location on a weaker one in another, as an ideal template to which the social reality of that place is commanded to conform. Moreover, political keywords are geographical in that they can seem fitting and/or benign as long as one keeps one's sights focused within the limits of the place in which they were first created but unfitting and/or malignant once one expands one's vision to include the spaces outside those parochial borders. Those foreign spaces may prove simply to lie outside the purview of the concept in question, quite innocently ignored by it, as the space of, say, the North Pole was outside and ignored by the French concept of fraternity. Or, they may lie outside the concept in appearance but in truth be a creature of that concept, as Said claimed that the space of the Orient was a creature of the Western concept of the Occident. Finally, they may lie outside the purview of the concept but become a casualty of actions animated by it, as Indian Country lay outside the geographical limits of the space within which the concept of government by the people, for the people was applied at the birth of the United States, but was gradually vanquished by the expansion of U.S. sovereign power across the continent.

Are global communication technologies subverting the geographical specificity of political language today? Given how quickly concepts travel as a result of the instantaneous electronic message, not to speak of how frequently people physically move, taking ideas with them, from place to place, the distinction between the inside and the outside, or the parochial and the foreign, seems on the way to becoming archaic. More implacably than the world-straddling but region-differentiating power of Western imperialism that preceded and paved the way for it, globalization is knitting the world tightly together. The conceptual effects of that knitting-together process are as of yet unclear. On the one hand, the shards and fragments of inherited ideas from all the world's peoples might become available to all, invigorating, in unpredictable and heterogeneous new mixtures, diverse efforts to come to terms with emergent realities. On the other hand, a global political vocabulary may subject everyone in the world to the same pre-determined range of possible thoughts and conceivable actions. But whether our future is multi- or univocal, "sovereignty" will not emerge unscathed. What will be—and should be—the fate of this concept, which long before the age of globalization had acquired the status of a nearly universal truth of exclusive political rule within a bounded territory, but which now is under universal strain?

The concept of sovereign power

After years of use as a relatively untroubled term of political discourse, "sovereignty" has come to agitate scholars of politics. In 1991 Nicholas Onuf explained the revitalized interest in this prominent but often taken-for-granted idea with respect to the international relations field.[8] In a spin on the notion that the owl of Minerva flies at dusk, he suggested that the concept becomes fully graspable only after it comes to actualization in the universalized form of the developed modern state—which is the very moment before the state form starts to buckle under the pressure of new conditions and political requirements. What once had seemed a permanent and self-evident background feature of political life becomes, in the age of sub- and supra-national competitors to the nation-state's agency and authority, a temporally limited and contingent question mark. As the sovereign state begins to lose even the semblance of the mastery over its affairs that impermeable boundaries around its territory once had been said to guarantee, political thinkers are provoked to inquire: When *did* sovereign power first emerge, what possibilities of thought and action are encouraged and inhibited by it, what should or will replace it, and, by the way, what exactly does "sovereignty" mean?

But other obstacles blocked a critical or even bemused attitude toward the concept in much of the twentieth century besides the fact that the modern state had not yet been hit over the head with challenges to its power and sufficiency. As a reflection of institutional realities in the West crystallizing in the sixteenth and seventeenth centuries, when overlapping authorities over land and populations gave way to exclusive political authority inside a delineated space, the discipline of political science posited sovereign power as a central premise of modern ideal and empirical political life. Regions of the world that had not achieved sovereign control over their internal affairs or were not recognized as sovereign by other states either were considered by mainstream political scientists to be weak, dependent, and/or backward or were barely considered at all. Especially international relations realists took sovereignty for granted by commission, using sovereign states as their basic unit of analysis; especially normative political theorists took sovereignty for granted by omission, tacitly accepting sovereign states as setting the limits for the polities to which their principles of justice, citizenship, and community applied.[9] In short, what was to become a strange puzzle to scholars of politics by the turn of the twenty-first century was assumed before then to be an already- or still-to-be achieved telos of political organization. Exceptions to this rule do not undermine it. For example, those international relations specialists in the 1960s who looked forward to the eclipse of conflict among Western sovereign states as a result of European integration could not and perhaps did not mean to foreclose the inference that national sovereign power would be ratcheted up and reconstituted at the higher, regional level. To take a very different example from the political theory field, Hannah Arendt, who unlike other normative theorists insisted on tackling not only abstract political ideals but also actual historical upheavals, identified, in her 1951 *The Origins of Totalitarianism*, the crisis for the modern state posed by stateless and rootless popula-tions; however, she saw this as a crisis for the *nation*-state, not the *sovereign* state.[10] As we shall see, a decade later Arendt sent out brief but penetrating philosophical salvos against sovereign power, but they would not rattle the edifice of even the political theory field for almost another 30 years.

Then, too, in the post-World War II period, the divide between the capitalist and communist blocs was more salient for intellectuals on all points of the political spectrum than the divides among sovereign or aspiring sovereign states, even though the conflict between capitalism and communism could be viewed as one type of sovereignty contest. Thus the most controversial concepts at the height of the Cold War were not "sovereignty" and "sovereign power" but "totalitarianism" (its application to communist societies endorsed by the right and center, repudiated by the left), "exploitation" (its application to capitalist societies endorsed by the left, repudiated by the right and center), and "equality," "justice," and "freedom" (endorsed as values by all parties, but conceived in clashing ways).

Quite apart from the roles played in obscuring perplexities of sovereign power by the naturalization of the sovereign state, political science disciplinary strictures, and a bi-polar division of the world, specific ideological camps had and continue to have their own reasons to avoid those perplexities. For traditional conservatives, the sovereign state was a muscular necessity to be, not interrogated, but revered, obeyed, and fought for as the strongest bulwark against social disorder and a threatening outside world. Libertarians, in contrast, harped on the danger posed to individual freedom by national government as the commanding power in society, even though that government was needed to defend individuals from foreign commanding powers. But far from being driven to critique sovereign power itself, libertarians pitted against the idea of the sovereignty of the state the more funda-mental principle of the natural sovereignty of the individual. For free market liberals in general, the geographically limited sovereign state was seen as an aggravating brake on (if also a necessary instrument of) the geographically limitless search for private profits, while the sovereign individual was the uninspected first premise that justified the right of every individual owner of property to do whatever he, and later she, wanted in that search. For many philosophical liberals, sovereign state power over domestic society, properly organized and restrained, was thought to protect the private rights that, as Mill had asserted, were prerequisites of the freedom or sovereignty of the individual. The interests of any particular liberal state over against other sovereign states, however, were too embarrassing to contemplate except by liberal advocates of global governance, given the incongruity of national interests with the principle of the equal value of all individuals everywhere.

Until it was eclipsed, the Marxist left mimicked, in an upside down way, the moral universalism of philosophical liberals and the economism of free market liberals on the sovereignty question. On the one side, the solidarity of all the working people of the world was seen as the denouement of history, not the permanent division of human loyalties along nation-state lines. On the other side, clashing modes of production were more important than clashing state powers, *capitalist* countries the preoccupying enemy, not capitalist *countries* in the form of sovereign states. There was, to be sure, one world-historical upheaval that kept sovereignty on the left's radar screen through at least the 1960s: the anti-colonial struggle for national independence in Africa, Asia, and the Middle East. As nervous as they were about nationalism in general, most Marxists would have concurred with Daniel Philpott's later claim (if not with the idealist arguments he makes in support of it), that the achievement of sovereign independence by colonized peoples was historically progressive, completing the universalization of the modern sovereign state form.[11] Much like the contradiction between state sovereignty and liberal individualism, the contradiction between state sovereignty and Marxist internationalism was real, but especially with respect to the political emancipation of the Third World, it had to be carefully tiptoed around.

A few decades later, and with an entirely different mindset, the poststructuralist left denied outright the preeminence of sovereign power in modern life. Following Michel Foucault, poststructuralists asserted that the micro-operations of normalizing power in institutions and discursive practices dispersed throughout society produced individuals with desirable proclivities, habits, and traits that minimized the need for a centralized coercive power to keep unruly subjects in line. In tandem or overlapping with technologies of "governmentality" in state and society through which whole populations were ordered for their own good and individuals remade as self-regulating, responsible private selves, normalizing power was declared to have replaced literal monarchical power and to have trumped the importance of the metaphorical monarch in the form of legal prohibitions against specific kinds of acts.

Poststructuralists charged those who still thought of political power in sovereign terms with being hobbled by outdated political imagery. Ironically, however, by pointing to modalities of power that they believed had made sovereignty largely passé, they helped bring the concept out of commonsense use and into the critical limelight. World-shattering empirical events and circumstances at the turn of the new century also catapulted sovereign power to the fore, and, against poststructuralists' initial claim, exposed that power as a contemporary problem, not an anachronistic one.

Clearly, the most significant of these events and circumstances was the growing impact of globalization on the modern state form to which Onuf was partly referring. This was the impact of speeded up global communications and transportation; large-scale, long-distance population migrations triggered by civil wars, natural disasters, and the collapse of local economies; boundary-crossing ecological problems; transnational social movements, especially those championing universal human rights; and the evident need for new kinds of political institutions to cope with the rest. Most important, it included not only the expansion of capitalism beyond the boundaries of the nation-state (a process that began in the age of European imperialism) but also the ability of global capital to set the parameters in which all nation-states were forced to function. As a result of globalization, even strong states seemed to be on the cusp of losing control over their borders, their natural resources, their ability to generate wealth for their own people, their ability to sculpt the identity of those people, and their use of power to further their distinctive national ideals.

A more staccato series of events underscoring the perplexities of sovereign power to the opposite effect was the collapse of Soviet-style communism and the rise of new ethnonationalist movements in the old Soviet empire. The quest for independent statehood by ethnic groups that had been submerged in a multinational political unit at first seemed to confirm, especially to enemies of communism, the division of humanity into distinct ethnic groups with a natural aspiration for freedom and the sovereign state as the institutional actualization of that freedom. The problematic character of that aspiration and actualization, however, quickly became apparent, especially in the former Yugoslavia, another broken-up multinational communist state. The orchestrated violence against Bosnian Muslims by Serbian nationalists, followed by the orchestrated violence against Rwandan Tutsi by the Hutu Power movement in central Africa, suggested that ethnonational sovereignty might have its logical end point not in freedom but in discrimination, persecution, even genocide. That a struggle for sovereignty could signify freedom for one group and obliteration for another was intimated by other ethnonational conflicts that finally caught the world's eye in their own right rather than as surrogates for the capitalism/communism conflict.

Two other political responses to contemporary conditions have exemplified and amplified a related conundrum of popular sovereignty. The first response is the hostility of nativist majorities toward immigrants, minorities, and aliens in both Western and non-Western countries. This raises the question of whether popular sovereignty—an expansive democratic ideal when set against the foil of monarchical sovereignty and an exuberant democratic ideal when set against the foil of an impersonal liberal legal system—is also a negative, exclusivist ideal as soon as there is a reason to ask who counts as belonging to "the people" and who does not. The millions of people moving around the world in search of work, asylum, or a refuge from political violence most recently have provided that reason. The hostility of privileged citizens (privileged *because* citizens) to deracinated foreigners also raises the question of whether sovereignty as the power to decide who will inhabit the "life" and "death" zones of citizenship and statelessness is an expression not merely, as some critics propose, of a modern form of "monarchical" sovereign power (i.e. power wielded by the prince, the state as a separate institution over society, or the executive branch of government acting above the law),[12] but also of democratic sovereign power (i.e. power exerted via strong popular sentiment).[13]

The conundrum of an exclusivist popular sovereignty is intensified when we turn to a second popular response to current conditions: the claim to counter-sovereignty made by those at the mercy of exogenous economic, political, and military forces that threaten to dominate or destroy their way of life. This claim has been leveled most recently by native peoples fending off sovereign state power and/or international capitalist imperatives, weaker countries attempting to protect themselves from the imperious demands of stronger ones, and popular movements wishing to reshape their governments without outside interference. Human rights advocates and other progressives condemn the sovereign power of xenophobic majorities and defend the aspirations to sovereign power of vulnerable peoples, but what exactly makes the exclusivism of privileged citizenship a minus in the ledger of democracy, and the exclusivism of penetrated indigeneity a plus?

Finally, sovereign state power has been exposed as a contemporary problem by a single catastrophe inflicted on the mightiest sovereign state in the world, not by another state, but by a small, international group of militants who were sovereign, at least until that instant, over no one and nothing. On the one hand, the viability of sovereign state power per se and the international system resting on it seemed to come unhinged in a single day, while the vicarious pleasure that many people around the world felt at the spectacular political violence of 9/11 could be seen as a popular reaction against the aim of a single country to become a global Leviathan. On the other hand, the response of the United States executive branch—its declaration of an endless preventative war against terror, its waging an actual war against a weak sovereign state as a substitute for its shadowy antagonist, and its indefinite detention of enemy combatants, torture of prisoners, extra-legal surveillance of aliens, and policing of citizens exercising their individual rights of free speech and association—was unnervingly reminiscent of a tyrannical version of absolute monarchical rule, which liberals thought they had vanquished long ago and poststructuralists assumed had been supplanted by subtler power modalities.

Then again, in combination with the violence of masterless men in weak states, terrorist attacks on strong states could not help but prompt some to wonder whether "monarchical" sovereign power was in fact preferable not only to the absence of state power but also to the presence of liberal constitutional constraints. Once popular sovereignty had become what Edmund Morgan has called the reigning modern fiction of Western politics, only right-wing authoritarians went as far as to counter to it not simply the hidden fact of elite rule but the overt ideal of the absolute power of a single leader.[14] After 9/11, Anglo-American liberal democracy flirted with a watered-down version of the same decisive single leader ideal.[15] The declaration of an indefinite state of emergency, suspension of the law, and assumption of executive prerogative were either passively or actively consented to by many political officials, intellectuals, and ordinary Americans, who, being complicit in the attempt to resurrect "monarchical" sovereign power, could not have been viewed as simple victims had that resurrection been entirely successful.[16]

In sum, sovereignty has emerged in our time as a highly complex and often incongruous knot of problems. There is the problem of the modern state's sovereignty over a bounded territory that is still the premise of institutional politics but is increasingly out of synch with economic, environmental, social, cultural, moral, and political forces, both local and global. There is the problem of the bleeding of searches for sovereign self-determination on the part of either threatened majorities or oppressed minorities into projects of sovereign domination. There is the problem of how to assess the exclusivist tendencies of popular sovereignty as a democratic ideal of rule and indigenous sovereignty as a weapon of the weak. There is the problem of "monarchical" sovereign power as an always latent possibility in politics that can and some say should be activated even in liberal democracies in response to catastrophic events and dangerous enemies. There is, finally, one other problem that has vexed many contemporary scholars of politics. What happens to sovereign power as it drains away from the modern state, to the extent that it does drain away? When it flows out of the nation-state, does it flow into some other container? Does it reappear as the deterritorialized, fractured, and networked powers of inter-linked global cities, transnational corporations, non-governmental organizations, and supranational institutions, as Saskia Sassen and John Agnew assert?[17] Does it become the diffuse quality of a world-straddling empire, with no outside, no unified center, and a logic that is inclusivist, not exclusivist, as Hardt and Negri contend?[18] Is capital itself an emerging global sovereign, as Wendy Brown suggests in *Walled States, Waning Sovereignty*: a sovereign that is no longer decisionist or centered on the friend/enemy distinction but still is "perpetual, absolute, and unifying" and "the source of all commands"?[19] Or is sovereignty dissolving altogether as a meaningful category of political life? And if it is, should we celebrate or regret its death?

Sovereign longings

Even those who anticipate a "post-sovereignty" age would hardly be as foolish as to deny the appeal of the sovereignty idea for much of the world today. To be convinced of that appeal for those who have actually enjoyed membership in a sovereign state as well as for those who still aspire to it, one need only cast a glance at the prickliness of each European state at any specific resolution of the European debt crisis that could be imposed upon it, the anger of Pakistanis at U.S. military incursions on their soil, even the jealousy with which the governor of Texas fends off what he sees as federal infringements on his state's sovereign rights, not to speak of all the bloody struggles for sovereign control over various corners of the earth.[20] A longing for sovereign power clearly continues to haunt contemporary politics, but what exactly incites and explains this longing?

For one of the timeliest answers to that question, let us take a closer look at the core argument of *Walled States, Waning Sovereignty.* In this text, Wendy Brown represents the current obsession with building walls around, between, and within nation-states as a performance of sovereign potency in front of an audience of anxious citizens to make up for the state's actual loss of potency in the face of global capitalism, religiously sanctioned political violence, neoliberal privatization, and unstoppable cross-border flows of money, people, information, environmental catastrophes, and crime. If fenced-off territory was the pre-condition for the emergence of the early modern sovereign state, obsessive walling is a doomed defensive reaction against the late modern collapse of those fences. And because ever more barbed wire, concrete barriers, surveillance systems, and armed border guards are needed to repel what cannot be repelled, walling threatens to turn domestic political society from a home into a "penitentiary" for its increasingly insecure inhabitants.[21] Sovereign political power, in short, deteriorates, but in a self-mystifying way, as states indulge in the theatrics of wall-building so that vulnerable human beings may identify with their pseudo-strength and majesty.

Given her focus on sovereignty as the power to "delimit, protect, and repel"[22]—in short, to provide human beings with security from threats—it is apt that Brown turns to Sigmund Freud's *The Future of an Illusion* for insight into the psychodynamics of sovereign fantasies. Defining "illusion" as a belief founded on a wish, Freud explains the belief in God as a reaction against infantile helplessness, a wish for an omnipotent father who can protect his human children from alien natural and social forces, and who must be more fearsome than any actual father in order to be more fearsome than any of those forces but who also must be moved by parental love. If Brown echoes Karl Marx and Carl Schmitt in seeing the sovereign state as a secularized version of the religious illusion (although, as Marx once reminded us, the "political illusion" at least has the virtue of being closer to reality than its religious counterpart), she echoes Freud when she posits the desire for the sovereign state as a desire for a fearsome yet loving protector.

Brown's account of the investments of individuals in sovereign state security captures an important aspect of the longing for sovereign power today. However, it over-shadows other equally important aspects.

The first over-shadowed aspect appears fleetingly in Brown's list of the paradoxes of sovereignty. Brown rightly states that the concept signifies an a priori authority and a generated authority, the foundation of law and a power not subject to the law, absolute monarchical power and popular self-rule, a majesty that depends on the state's theological derivations and a majesty that frees itself from religious authority, domination within the nation-state and anarchy among states, the state's independence *vis-à-vis* other states and its dependence on them for their recognition of its independence. The play of domination and freedom in almost every entry in this list proves this political concept to be curiously double-valued, unlike political concepts that are unambiguously positive or negative, including "freedom" and "domination" themselves. Brown explains the longing for "negative" sovereign domination as the securing of the subject from outside threats, but why has sovereign power also been longed for as the "positive" route to and substance of freedom?

The second over-shadowed aspect has to do with the beginning, not the end, of sovereign power's trajectory. Brown remarks in passing that sovereign power "is identified with settled jurisdiction, not with settling it,"[23] but a new power must eradicate whatever power existed previously in a space in order to become sovereign over that space. To focus solely on either the operations or the decline of sovereign state power in its already settled space is to elide the violence of its founding as well as later erasures of that violence from collective memory that encourage the longing for sovereign power by casting its origins in a rosy glow. The foundational violence of sovereignty is not merely of historical interest with respect to the birth of the modern sovereign state form. It reappears at the birth of every new state, the territorial expansion of state authority, and political revolutions in established states—none of which has been consigned to the dustbin of history by the waning of sovereign power as of yet.

Finally, too singular focus on the fantastical quality of sovereign state power in the context of the twenty-first century obscures the ways in which sovereign power is fantastical in any context. As Brown notes, Freud defines an illusion as a belief founded in a wish. He reminds us that illusions "need not necessarily be false—that is to say, unrealizable or in contradiction with reality," providing the example of a middle-class girl who is under the illusion "that a prince will come and marry her."[24] Princes exist, and so does marriage, but it is highly unlikely, although not impossible, that princes will marry "girls" beneath their station. The analogy suggests that sovereign power has existed in the form of the modern state, as has the protection enjoyed by the state's subjects, but it is highly unlikely, although not impossible, that the state can provide the same protection in the future. But while the longing, ambition, and struggle for sovereign power are undeniably real, what if sovereign power itself is always a chimera? Freud defines "delusion," in contrast with "illusion," as a belief at odds with reality, in the way that (my example this time) a boy is deluded who is thinks he is talking to a mermaid. However, Freud admits that some illusions are so improbable that they resemble delusions, and he sometimes uses the two terms interchangeably in his metaphorical diagnoses of the illnesses of social and political life. His suggestion of beliefs that oscillate between illusions and delusions gives us license to ask not only "What is the wish at the center of the desire for sovereign power?" but also "To what extent does not just a specific historical circumstance but life itself make that wish impossible to fulfill?"

Before we can answer this question, we must tackle a more preliminary set. What is sovereign power imagined to be? Who is considered its rightful possessor? What goods is it believed to supply, and who is deemed the beneficiary of those goods? If we consult the tradition of Western political thought, where the theory of sovereignty originates, we will find, perhaps unsurprisingly, that answers to these questions after the rise of the idea of modern democracy break in important ways with answers before yet also contain a strong residue of those earlier answers. More surprisingly, as this book will try to show, the discrepancy between the longing for sovereign power and not just a particular historical reality but reality *per se*, as well as the dangers inherent in that discrepancy, is exaggerated, not ameliorated, when the concept of sovereign power is democratized.

Classical monarchical sovereign power

Two of the greatest pre-democratic theorists of sovereign power are Jean Bodin, the sixteenth-century "father" of the concept of absolute monarchical sovereignty, and Thomas Hobbes, who in the seventeenth century grounds monarchical absolutism not in a pre-existing social hierarchy but in the natural equality of all human beings.

Sovereign power as Bodin construes it is the absolute and perpetual power to command, which he rather chillingly describes as follows. To be sovereign is to have the power to give the law to subjects but not be subject to that law, to give the law to subordinates without their consent, to make law that is "nothing but the command of a sovereign making use of his power."[25] It is to be the lord of everything and possess everything in governance, to rule in the image of God, to recognize nothing but God that is greater than oneself. From the sovereign prerogative of law-making, all other prerogatives of sovereignty are extrapolated: overriding or repealing or clarifying the law, attaching rewards and punishments to the law, making peace and declaring war, instating and removing high officers and magistrates of state, levying taxes on subjects but exempting those one pleases, hearing appeals in the last instance, pardoning persons who deserve to die, accepting fealty and homage, coining money and regulating weights and measures, having rights to the sea, compelling a change in language in society, and enjoying the title of majesty.

While Bodin acknowledges that a select group (an aristocracy) or a whole people (a democracy) can be sovereign, he sees monarchy as the form of commonwealth that best instantiates the unitary and centralized nature of sovereign power. Thus the most fitting possessor of sovereign power is the single person of the Prince. The good that sovereign power supplies is in large part a good for him. We can infer that good from the keywords with which Bodin associates the concept of sovereignty: greatness, lordship, majesty, authority, grandeur, mastery, being the highest human source of command and prohibition. In a nutshell, the good of sovereign power for the Prince is such recognized superiority that he can impose his will on society without encountering inside that society the legitimate or effective opposition of another human will.[26]

Remarkably, however, to anyone looking at things from a post-eighteenth-century perspective, sovereign power does not supply the Prince with the good of freedom. Bodin not only fails to exult in the sovereign freedom of the monarch; he rarely links freedom and sovereignty together. The concept closest to "freedom" on which he regularly draws is "liberty," but this refers to the rights and privileges not of the Prince but of particular subjects, estates, churches, and other non-state institutions. As for the Prince, because he is the image of God, he must model his laws "on the law of God" and make sure that those laws have justice as their end. The Prince may be "answerable only to God," but he is more "strictly bound than any of his subjects" to obey the laws of God and nature.[27] Far from enjoying freedom in the sense of doing whatever one wants or even doing whatever one wants as long as one does not injure others, and far from enjoying freedom in the different sense of being self-determining instead of being at the mercy of forces outside one's control, Bodin's Prince occupies a defined place, albeit the highest human place, in a great hierarchy of places, each hemmed in by its requisite restrictions and obligations. In addition to being compelled to obey the will of God, who is the "highest sovereign," the Prince is compelled, as a monarch, not a despot, to respect the private liberty of his subjects. He cannot take away their possessions at his pleasure, he cannot tax them without their consent, and he is bound by all the just private contracts and promises he has made with other persons. The good of sovereign power for the Prince is thus the unmatched and unquestioned superiority of his will over every other human will, not a free range of desire and action. The combination of its superiority and moral substance explains why sovereign power has, as a second beneficiary, the Prince's subjects, for whom its good is a just and peaceful social order.

Although Hobbes endorses the ideal of absolute sovereign power and monarchy as its most perfect institutional form, he is aligned in the egalitarian premises from which he deduces this political conclusion more with the democratic theorists who come after him than with theorists of monarchical absolutism who come before. His first premise is the principle of the natural liberty of every individual to use his own power as he chooses to preserve himself, with a natural right to everything that he sees as a means to that end. The free pursuit of those things brings these individuals insecurity, conflict, and the threat of early death, because three other egalitarian premises also hold true: that every man is roughly equal in mental and physical capacities, or, by uniting with others, could become equal to one who is momentarily superior; that every man is driven by restless and infinite desire, especially the desire for power to gain everything else that he desires; and that every other man represents a force to fear, either as a competitor for the same object of desire or because he may have desires that clash with one's own, as a man whose desire for territorial aggrandizement might clash with another man's desire for a tranquil and secure little home. While the combination of desire and fear prompts all men to "love Liberty, and Dominion over others," the natural equality of men guarantees that no one can enjoy the fruits of either good for long. Hobbes's solution to the ills of the state of nature is an artificial Commonwealth or State with the punitive power to secure a commodious life for all by forcing each of its members to act according to the golden rule, *"Do not that to another, which thou wouldest not have done to thy selfe."*[28] States may be established by the joint consent of individuals, as in Commonwealths by Institution, or they may be established by the violent force of a single man or group, as in Commonwealths by Acquisition, but in both cases the essential impetus to and operations of sovereign power are exactly the same.

The individual forfeits his will to the Sovereign to safeguard him from the threats that other men pose, by promising to obey the Sovereign's law except where it would destroy his life. In return, he has the liberty to do what he has the desire and ability to do wherever the law is silent.

In the state of nature the individual aspired to a commanding will but could not attain it. In political society he gives up the aspiration. On the other side of the command equation, in political society Hobbes's monarch possesses almost all the sovereign prerogatives that Bodin's does, and many that he doesn't, including the power to determine what is just and unjust. Hobbes's monarch not only is unbound by the laws he makes for society; individuals, estates, and institutions have no rights and privileges that do not derive from him. At points in the text, he does not seem to be subordinated to any supra-human authority, even though he might cloak his own authority in the guise of the divine. All of this might suggest that the monarch is not only sovereign but also absolutely free in Hobbes's sense of the term, acting according to nothing other than his own will and facing no obstructions in his way. And yet there would be something very odd about portraying the aim of monarchical power as sovereign freedom. What was a flesh and blood Prince for Bodin becomes much more of an institutional device for Hobbes, "an Artificiall *Soul*" of an "Artificiall Man," with no passions or pleasures of its own that could be furthered by the unlimited freedom to pursue them.[29] Indeed, sovereign power exists solely to prohibit men from giving *their* passions free reign, by covering them with an umbrella of positive law that makes effectual the eternal laws of nature, including the imperatives of mutual accommodation, equity, humility, promise-keeping, and so on, so that each man, in obeying the law, can trust that all other men will be punished if they do not do the same. Moreover, while Hobbes sometimes suggests that the laws of nature are simply prudential dictates of reason, he sometimes suggests that they are moral laws designed and bestowed on man by God. In either case, the monarch himself is "as much subject, as any of the meanest of his People" to those same natural laws, and his positive laws must function to give earthly potency to them.[30] If, then, as a natural and universal human attribute, "liberty" plays a larger initial role in Hobbes's theory than in Bodin's, where it is the limited product of traditional right, Hobbes no less than Bodin refrains from equating liberty with sovereign power, which he posits instead as a separate, opposed, and circumscribing force.

What does it mean to dream of sovereign power as Bodin and Hobbes understand the term, given that it does not mean to dream of sovereign freedom? It could mean to wish to possess such superiority of will over all other human wills that one can impose on them one's vision, whether divinely inspired or not, of a just and peaceable social order (and how many of us have not had *that* fantasy from time to time!). Alternatively, it could mean to wish to inhabit a just and peaceable social order, compliments of someone else's superior will.

Is this desire for an absolute but benevolent authoritarianism an illusion compatible with reality—or is it utterly fantastical? Certainly, history is full of tales of powerful rulers who maintain a kind of peace, and possibly a kind of justice, by imposing order on whole populations. But what turns out to be a chimera is not simply, as every student of politics is taught, a perpetual and absolute power that does not eventually corrupt the human being who wields it and undo whatever justice he or she had installed. The chimera is, more fundamentally, the idea of a power that is perpetual and absolute, for this idea entails that the wills of all other human beings can be not merely cowed but permanently crushed. If Nietzsche is right that where there is life, there is will (and surely he *is* right), then sovereign power, which requires live subjects, is destined to meet up eventually with resistance, disobedience, defiance, and even aggressive bids to counter-sovereignty, whether out of anger at specific substantive injustices wrought by sovereign power, resentment at the sovereign's monopolization of will-power, or conviction that any monopolization of will-power is unjust. Indeed, it is one of the self-defeating traits of sovereign power that it often sparks desires for counter-sovereignty even among those who originally had not seen the world in sovereignty terms. But whether or not those subjected to sovereign power come to desire sovereign power for themselves (instead of, say, the right to live in non-sovereign communion with the world or have a voice equal with all other voices in public affairs), the stubbornly resilient quality of the human will, in combination with the shifts in circumstance that inevitably bring ruin on all ambitions to permanence, makes power over the wills of others always an incomplete and ephemeral achievement.

Sovereign freedom

In hindsight, it is predictable that sovereign power would become associated with freedom *as opposed to* domination once resistance to monarchical power was mounted in earnest. By "monarchical power" I mean not only the power of a king who rules over individual subjects in his territory but also, following Hobbes's allusion to imperialism, the power of a whole people that, however it is ruled itself, rules another people elsewhere always as their monarch.[31] In the case of literal monarchical power, the association between sovereignty and freedom developed in Europe, from the seventeenth century on, as rising elites who had been pressing their literal monarchs for an expansion of their liberties begin to cast their eye on their monarchs' thrones; as popular classes, once called by elites onto the stage for a silent role in politics as "the people," began to covet the privileges and growing political power of those elites; and as royal power and traditional social hierarchies were finally overthrown in popular revolutions or fatally degraded by democratic reforms.[32] In the case of metaphorical monarchical power, the association between sovereignty and freedom intensified in the late eighteenth, nineteenth, and twentieth centuries, as European powers were ejected from their overseas colonies by movements for political independence or national liberation, as nationalities in disintegrating multinational empires clamored for their own sovereign states, and as oppressed minorities in nation-states struggled against national majorities for political autonomy. Most recently, that association has reappeared wherever popular masses demand national sovereignty against foreign interfering powers and popular sovereignty against domestic dictators and corrupt ruling elites.

In short, attaining freedom from monarchical power, which in real life proved more oppressive than Bodin and Hobbes theorized, has seemed to people in many centuries and many regions to be synonymous with wresting the prerogatives of sovereign power for themselves. To command instead of being commanded, to possess an effectual will instead of meekly bowing to a master, to control the conditions of one's existence instead of being at the mercy of alien forces, to shine with the dignity of a sovereign self instead of living in the shadow of another's grandeur, to corral the state to serve one's own needs and interests instead of being exploited or neglected by those who monopolize state power: these desires have proved so compelling that, except for a few intellectual skeptics, sovereignty today is widely seen as the prerequisite and inner substance of a freely lived life. The modern association of sovereign power and freedom in fact has become so ingrained that it crops up in the thinking of those nostalgic for monarchical absolutism such as Carl Schmitt, who sees the highest virtue of sovereign power as the ability to break with the torpor of bureaucratic routine, decide the exception to the law, and partake in the "miracle" of free action.[33] The sovereignty/freedom nexus is even tighter for those who, on behalf of the sovereign freedom of the individual, reject sovereign state power in *either* its popular or monarchical form.

If in practice the idea of sovereign power metamorphosed into sovereign freedom as part of complicated and prolonged historical processes, in theory the metamorphosis most famously occurs in a more punctuated way, in a few passages of a single eighteenth-century text.[34] Against Hobbes and other absolute monarchists for whom the human race is "divided into herds of cattle, each with a master who preserves it only in order to devour its members," Jean-Jacques Rousseau poses the central question of *The Social Contract*: " 'How to find a form of association which will defend the person and goods of each member with the collective force of all, and under which each individual, while uniting himself with the others, obeys no one but himself, and remains as free as before.'" His answer still reverberates throughout the world today. To be free in political society, human beings must be equal members of "an artificial and collective body," who "take collectively the name of *a people,* and call themselves individually *citizens,* in so far as they share in the sovereign power, and *subjects,* in so far as they put themselves under the laws of the state." No less faithfully than Hobbes, Rousseau follows Bodin in defining sovereign power as the capacity to command and not be commanded. Against Bodin, Rousseau asserts that a "people, since it is subject to laws, ought to be the author of them."[35] Against Hobbes, who posits, at least in sovereign power by institution, the people as authors of all the sovereign does but sharply separates sovereign agency from the individuals who author it and are subjected to it, Rousseau secures the freedom of each man in political society by apportioning to him an equal share of authorship of sovereign power, the exercise of sovereign will, and the obligation to obey the laws that the popular sovereign makes.

Against the backdrop of actual monarchical regimes, the elimination of the divide between the subject and object of political power was such a breath of fresh air that the dangers in associating sovereign power with freedom were difficult for many critics of monarchy to see. Most of the worries that surfaced about what Etienne Balibar has called "the perilous leap to popular sovereignty"[36] concerned not sovereign freedom but the General Will. Rousseau believed that, to enter political society as an equal member of the sovereign body, each individual had to exchange his "natural liberty" to act on instinct, impulse, and appetite for moral reason, "which alone makes man the master of himself; for to be governed by appetite alone is slavery, while obedience to a law one prescribes to oneself is freedom."[37] It is only, however, when each citizen wills the General Will or what he believes is the common good, instead of willing what is in his interest as a private ego, that the laws that are made by the sovereign people as a whole will confirm the freedom of the individual instead of restricting or denying it.

Early on, elites who made use of the rhetoric of popular sovereignty suspected the General Will of being a class mechanism by which the property-less would trample over propertied interests. Later, liberals denounced its totalitarian threat to unique individuals with diverse opinions, multiculturalists disclosed its repressive implications for plural social groups, and agonistic democratic theorists pointed out its impossibility given the dynamic and fissiparous character of political life. In fact, however, the idea of a general will—that which one wills when one puts aside one's special individual or group interests to think of the good of society as a whole, including the good of oneself as a member of that whole—has much more going for it from a democratic perspective than the idea of sovereign freedom. To will what one believes is good for all, not just good for oneself as a separated entity, may be merely a hypocritical exercise of disguising one's self-interest as the general interest or dressing up one's circumscribed life conditions as the superior way of life that everyone else should be forced to endure. But it also may be, very differently, an exercise in empathetic identification with a wider network of sentient and even non-sentient beings. As such, the General Will is humanly capacious. When it contests rather than expresses sovereign power, it also can be admirably courageous. For its capacious quality, think of Western environmentalists' will to curtail their own commodity consumption out of a concern for the fate of the planet as a whole. For its courageous quality, think of the spontaneous general wills of the Tunisian, Egyptian, and Syrian peoples during the Arab Spring uprisings—general wills that were unprotected, un-sovereign challenges to monarchical sovereign power "from the street."

To aspire to sovereign power as the route to freedom is quite another, more self-referential and, for all other wills, much less appetizing thing. That such an aspiration could belong to an entire people instead of a would-be autocrat seems relatively unimportant from any outsider perspective. Certainly an entire people that desires sovereign freedom ought to be, from such a perspective, at least as unsettling as a single individual who desires sovereign power in the classical Bodinian or even Hobbesian sense. This is true partly because no individual can do too much harm without large numbers of others behind him, while large numbers can do a great deal of harm without an autocratic leader. But it is more importantly true because a people that attained absolute sovereign freedom (if sovereign freedom proves to be something that *can* be attained) would be, unlike Bodin's and Hobbes's sovereign monarchs, entirely unrestricted, not only in how it acted but also in what it willed, by any kind of law superior to itself that could impose justice on its relationships with others. Ironically, the worst case relation of popular sovereign freedom to outsiders is an upside down image of the worst-case relation of the classical monarch towards those thought to be beyond the protection of even God's law. In the case of the classical monarch: "God, the highest sovereign, commands me, as his servant and your master, to persecute heretics and kill unbelievers." In the case of popular sovereign freedom: "if there is no God, everything we wish to do to you is permitted."

To be fair to Rousseau, his theory establishes all sorts of hedges against many of popular sovereignty's dangers to those outside the parameters of "the people." These hedges include a universal law of justice accessible to natural reason; the human sentiment of compassion for others that is rooted in an animal capacity for pity; the prescription of a small, self-sufficient, materially modest polity that would have no economic impulse to aggress against other regions; and a call for the tolerance of other peoples with different religious beliefs. But Rousseau mainly was preoccupied with how a self-governing people could be made out of independent individuals and how relations among individual members of a single people could be both just and free, rather than with what the consequences might be of one people's sovereign power for individual strangers, ethnic minorities, and other peoples, not to speak of other species of being, especially if his theoretical hedges around popular sovereign freedom collapsed in practice. In this respect, at least, Edmund Burke came closer to acknowledging practical realities when he remarked that while sufferers from monarchical cruelty at least can "assuage the smart of their wounds" with the "balmy compassion of mankind," those "subjected to wrong under multitudes" are "deprived of all external consolation" and seem "deserted by mankind."[38]

It has been tempting for many democrats to evade the dangerous consequences of sovereign freedom by distinguishing between two types of sovereign power: a "bad," dominative type that is exercised by, to borrow a phrase from Tom Nairn, big battalions, and a "good," emancipatory type that is exercised by small battalions. Internationally, this "big bad/small good" distinction lines up with the difference between rich states and poor ones, neo-imperialist powers and weaker regions, and actual states and states that exist only in the political imagination of some downtrodden group. Domestically, it lines up with the difference between upper classes and popular masses, amoral dictators and oppressed subjects, arrogant ethnic majorities and perse-cuted minorities, and settler and indigenous races. On the border between the international and the domestic, it lines up with the difference between chauvinistic citizens and stateless populations. But if I might borrow another phrase that Nairn used with respect to nationalist movements: are there *really* black and white cats here, or are all cats spotted, without exception?

For a perceptive answer to this question, let us turn to Hannah Arendt's essay, "What is freedom?" Here Arendt traces the roots of the idea of sovereign freedom to the Augustinian notion of free will, or a will that wills only what the self wills it to will, which in Augustine's case meant the will to direct desire to things of the spirit instead of things of the flesh. According to Arendt, the identification of freedom with the will's capacity to determine its desires eventually migrates from the inner psychological realm of a self's spiritual struggle with itself to the outer secular political realm, where it metamorphoses into the "pernicious and dangerous" idea of sovereign freedom as a self-determining will "independent from others and eventually prevailing against them."[39] Conversely, it is only after secularization— in the maximal sense of the liberation of the human subject from divine authority or the minimal sense of its liberation from a divinely imposed human authority—that the subject can see itself as having not merely freedom of the will but sovereign freedom. The self who is liberated from divine authority is free to desire and will and do exactly what he wishes instead of what some metaphysical entity dictates that he *should* desire and will and do. The self who is liberated from a divinely invested human authority can command himself politically as he sees fit, being no longer morally compelled to bow down to a human superior, even if he chooses to bow down to what he sees as his sovereign God. In either case, however, the secular self enjoys sovereign freedom only theoretically. In practice, he can determine himself freely only if he gains control of all the worldly conditions that otherwise would condition or limit him.

What makes the idea of sovereign freedom a delusion in Arendt's eyes is not the truth of the existence of a supreme spiritual power or an earthly sovereign power anointed by it. It is the very different truth that "not man but men live on the earth."[40] Under the condition of human plurality, the identification of freedom with sovereignty implies either that no one in the world can be free, because no one has control over all the other wills that might otherwise affect him against his will, or that only a single self can be free as a result of having crushed the capacity for freedom of every other human being. Against the absurdity that freedom is either a mirage or a synonym for tyranny, Arendt discards the idea of sovereign freedom altogether. She re-conceptualizes freedom as worldly and political, not a function of the psychological state of the individual and the determination of its will. She hinges freedom not on the absence of any pressure on the self from other selves, but on the release of individuals from a narrow social enclosure to a more expansive "common public sphere," where they are able "to get away from home, to go into the world and meet other people," inserting themselves in the wider world "by word and deed."[41] She describes freedom as the capacity of anyone (not just Schmitt's modern monarch) to begin something new, to partake in the miracle of action by interrupting automatic processes such as the cyclical maintenance of biological life, the repetition of custom, bureaucratic routine, or seemingly inevitable chains of causes and effects. Consequently, freedom grows in the world to the extent that a greater and greater number of individuals can start something new that can be responded to by other individuals each in his or her distinctive way; it shrinks in the world to the extent that a smaller and smaller number can dictate the responses of others to their own initiatives. The fact that total control over others is impossible to achieve explains why "the famous sovereignty of political bodies has always been an illusion." The fact that those who dream of that impossibility must use coercion against the wills of others to try to make their dream real explains why that illusion, or delusion, can be maintained "only by the instruments of violence." In short, sovereign freedom defeats freedom on two counts. The self that aspires to it must seek to deny others the delights of free action and chain *itself* to the implacable imperatives of an unrealizable project. Therefore, "if men wish to be free, it is precisely sovereignty they must renounce."[42]

Arendt's "anti-sovereignty" conceptualization of freedom as the capacity to begin something new but not to determine what happens afterwards has been dismissed as elitist and abstract.[43] Its real drawback, however, is the concept's one-sided emphasis on new beginnings at the expense of patterns that have congealed out of new beginnings, making up a style of existence to which one has become attached.[44] This drawback will be obvious to anyone who ever has been forced by others to forfeit not only deeply satisfying practices and social relations but also a particular landscape in the way it has been collectively shaped and used. Thus we would do well to expand Arendt's idea of freedom to incorporate not just the capacity for new beginnings but also the capacity to perpetuate a beloved way of life, for as long as it *is* beloved, on the condition that it does not demand the participation of those who do not enjoy it, does not exclude those who do, does not foreclose the possibility that differently enjoyable ways of life may be lived elsewhere, and has not established itself by destroying a different way of life that has met those same conditions. The benefit of understanding freedom in terms of the twin capacities of beginning and perpetuating can be seen as soon one tries to imagine a life in which one is constantly beginning something new but never able to enjoy any recognizable pattern of life, or in which one is constantly repeating familiar patterns without ever being able to escape them.

While equally valuable, the capacities for breaking with and preserving the given differ in other ways than their substantive difference. Creativity is more often associated with the individual person, and the enjoyment of a way of life with the collective, even though it is individuals who do the enjoying and collectivities that are most dramatically jolted by new beginnings—sometimes so dramatically that the collectivity mutates or disintegrates as a consequence. Then, too, domestic sovereign power usually poses the greater threat to the capacity to begin something new, and foreign sovereign power the greater threat to familiar patterns of existence. Finally, the desire for collective counter-sovereignty, often although not always manifested in the desire for control of a state and territory, is more likely to be felt by those whose way of life is threatened by a foreign or at least culturally alien sovereign power than by those whose creative ventures are threatened by a domestic or native sovereign power, perhaps because the security that one's own sovereign state promises dovetails with the capacity to preserve what is and clashes with the miracle of action. For all these reasons, the question of whether successful counter-sovereignty struggles can avoid the pernicious consequences of winning sovereign power is most pertinent for those who are defending their freedom in the collective, preservative sense of the term.

Heinz Lubasz once drew a strict line between sovereign power and the total domination of twentieth-century totalitarian regimes.[45] Arendt's "What is Freedom?" suggests that they are, to the contrary, points along the same continuum. Although she does not differentiate them explicitly, we can infer from her line of argument three impulses to domination that infect every search for freedom as the capacity to act "with final authority" and "irresistible power"[46] over against a competitor or antagonist. The first is the impulse to self-domination.

We have seen how Rousseau believed that the self must achieve mastery over its own appetites and instincts instead of being mastered by them, in order to become a self in sovereign control of itself. But the more pertinent point for us is that a self that is initially, to steal another phrase from Freud, polymorphous perverse—open to the entire world in its potential identifications with others—must hammer itself or be hammered into a self whose identifications are more restricted and exclusive, before it can have a reason to wish for sovereign freedom as opposed to and over against something that it sees as not-itself. With respect to the wish for the sovereign freedom of the human species, the self must identify with the human species in distinction from and over against all other varieties of being, be they mineral, vegetable, animal, or metaphysical. With respect to the wish for national sovereign freedom, the self must identify with a single people in distinction from and over against all other peoples. With respect to the wish for individual sovereign freedom, the self must identify with a single self—itself—in distinction from and over against other individuals. In sum, the search for sovereign freedom can be initiated only by a self that has already cut potential ties of identification with other entities in the world, or has had its ties cut by others, for it is only then that those other entities become alien beings over against which the self believes that its sovereign freedom must be fought for and won.

The second impulse to domination that animates the search for sovereign freedom is the self's drive to dominate everything outside itself in the physical space that it inhabits, for every embodied self (whether individual or collective) will be pressured and limited by the alien objects it habitually encounters and so will be unable to attain sovereign freedom unless it masters them. This includes mastering, within its habitat, brute-physical objects, other living species of being, and other human subjects who are seen as alien to the self, or who see the self as alien to themselves, or both.

The third impulse to domination that animates the search for sovereign freedom is the self's drive to dominate other objects (especially objects that are other subjects) outside its place of habitation, because, at a greater distance, those objects also represent, whether as a looming presence (such as another state) or a missing absence (such as a needed resource), a potential pressure or limit on the self. Only by controlling the whole world, in the end, can the self be assured of commanding without being commanded by any other will, determining the content of its own will, and acting according to that will without external obstruction.

The impossibility of sovereign freedom under the condition of human plurality, as well as the degeneration of self–other relations to which every attempt to make the impossible possible testifies, has not prevented desires for sovereign freedom from working their black magic on modern politics. The cases featured in Chapters 2 and 3 illustrate that black magic's deleterious effects on freedom in our expanded Arendtian sense of the term. Chapter 2 considers how "the greatest experiment on earth" to institute popular sovereignty and individual freedom against the grain of royal power and fixed social hierarchies was contingent on the violent erasure of life worlds that had been no less popularly and freely enjoyed. Chapter 3 considers how a struggle to free a religious minority from "the greatest persecution on earth" by allotting that minority sovereignty over a new corner of the earth precipitated another persecution.

These case studies do not pretend to be definitive histories of their subjects. Instead, they are efforts to reveal, through highly distilled portraits of two of its many empirical manifestations, the paradoxical logic of a modern political idea. Both in deference to the political theoretical agenda of this book and because the concept of sovereignty is entangled with other key concepts, we will open our first case with a spotlight on "foundational violence" and close our second case with a requiem to "national self-determination."

2

Foundational Violence and the Politics of Erasure

Foundational violence

[T]he lawgivers and founders of mankind ... all of them to a man were criminals, from the fact alone that in giving a new law they thereby violated the old one, held sacred by society and passed down from their fathers, and they certainly did not stop at shedding blood either, if it happened that blood (sometimes quite innocent and shed valiantly for the ancient law) could help them—Raskolnikov

The violence involved in the formation of political orders makes a fascinating footnote to Western political thought. I use the word "footnote," because, unlike historians who are drawn to the tumult in which new ideas and practices emerge, political theorists tend to spill their ink on what they see as ideal political norms and institutions, not on the grittier processes by which actors impose norms and establish institutions in attempts to make the ideal real. Even social contract theorists, who do pay special attention to the moment of political founding, attend to it in an abstract and antiseptic form, representing that moment not as an occasion for violence but as the point at which consent, reason, justice, and law substitute for bloodshed in human affairs. Additionally, whether or not they accept the notion of a social contract, political theorists who are enamored of liberal principles often soft-pedal or efface the violence at the birth of political societies that are now proudly liberal democratic, not to speak of the violence that can be said, and has been said by critics, to covertly and at times overtly animate those same societies.[1]

Notwithstanding such diffidence towards political violence in the normative political theory field, vivid allusions to the violent creation and regulation of cities, states, and empires are scattered throughout the history of political thought from the ancient period to our own. Political order, Augustine notes early on in that history, has the function of enforcing relations of mastery and obedience and punishing men whose sinful desires lead them to commit crimes against other men, yet it is itself born out of a great disobedience and a great crime. The first "earthly city" was founded by Cain, who out of the "diabolical, envious hatred with which the evil regard the good" had slain his brother Abel, a "citizen of the eternal city, and a sojourner on earth." Given that the very founder of political foundings was stained with his brother's blood, "we cannot be surprised," Augustine writes, "that this first specimen, or, as the Greeks say, archetype of crime, should, long afterwards, find a corresponding crime at the foundation of that city which was destined to reign over so many nations."[2] Driven by egotism and ambition to compete for the glory of founding Rome, Romulus and Reus demonstrate to Augustine not the division of the city of man against the city of God but the division of the earthly city against itself. Thus, if the first fratricide highlights the fallen nature of man that makes punitive political societies necessary, the second symbolizes the crime that all new political societies commit by dividing members of the human race into separate and antagonistic peoples.[3]

A no less vivid reference to the violent founding of states (followed by "nothing but acts of violence" afterwards) appears in Nietzsche's *On the Genealogy of Morals*. Here, violence is a matter not of fratricide but of violation-and-creation. Nietzsche evokes this doublet with the images of a beast of prey that "unhesitatingly lays its terrible claws upon a populace perhaps tremendously superior in numbers but still formless and nomad," an egoistic artist who hammers into shape a "hitherto unchecked and shapeless populace," and "an oppressive and remorseless machine" that kneads the "raw material of people and semi-animals" into a social group that is "firm" and "pliant."[4] All three images convey both the privative and the productive aspects of foundational violence: its assault on the anarchic freedom of unorganized human life, and its welding together a specific people out of unrelated elements.

If we join Augustine's and Nietzsche's points, we can say that each new political society entails two violent moments that occur simultaneously and as a function of one another. A distinctive form is imposed on a human mass, and the people corralled under that form are differentiated and dissociated from all other people, who become their potential enemies. Although Nietzsche and Augustine in his Cain and Abel story are referring to the birth of the first political societies, the logics they describe also apply to the formation of all political societies after that. In the latter cases, new collective forms are imposed not on sheer human formlessness but on previous collectives, and new fratricides occur with respect to, not the rest of the human race, but some sub-set of it with which the members of the new collective once had been but no longer are united.

The birth of a new political order is the birth not only of a people but also of a new authority that will rule over them. That violence is the basis of political authority is a precept Max Weber underscores in "Politics as a Vocation," where, while no friend of the Bolsheviks, he seconds Leon Trotsky's pronouncement that "[e]very state is founded on force." Weber goes on to define political institutions as relations of "men dominating men" and the modern state as men dominating men while monopolizing the right to use force in doing so, even though it does not always or even normally exercise that right. But if the modern state is "a human community that (successfully) claims the *monopoly of the legitimate use of physical force* within a given territory," it is only the superiority of its amassed might that allows the state to make that claim effectual.[5] Thus we are left to wonder what gives any greater concentration of power the *right*, not simply the might, to deny the right of violence to all lesser concentrations.

The insufficiency of force as a ground for political authority explains why political power invariably tries to root itself in a moral or prudential principle of some sort. Nevertheless, regardless of how overwhelming the might that paved the way for it or how assiduously it claims after the fact to be expressive of divine right, natural reason, or some other higher law, political authority is, when it first comes into being, unauthorized. In his ruminations on Walter Benjamin's "Critique of Violence," Jacques Derrida evokes this paradox of political authority when he asks: "How to distinguish between the force of law ... of a legitimate power and the allegedly originary violence that must have established this authority and that could not itself have authorized itself by an anterior legitimacy?" Authority that establishes itself as legitimate has at its origin no right to do so, since right does not create authority but is created by it. "Since the origin of authority, the founding or grounding ... the positing of the law ... cannot by definition rest on anything but themselves, they are themselves a violence without ground."[6] State foundings, that is, are violent, not in being bloody (although they may be bloody), but in inaugurating authoritative power without the authority to do so.

Derrida's notion of the unauthorized creation of authority bears a family resemblance to Nietzsche's notion of the coercive creation of a people, in that both connote an act of sheer power that comes, so to speak, out of nowhere. But is there an object that must be violated to pave the way for a new authoritative law, as raw human material had to be violated to pave the way for a civilized population, or as one politically organized people had to be violated to pave the way for another? Derrida means to showcase the productive aspect of violence when he declares: "The foundation of all states ... inaugurates a new law; it always does so in violence. *Always*, which is to say even when there have not been those spectacular genocides, expulsions or deportations that so often accompany the foundation of states, great or small."[7] Yet, if the "always" in the last sentence dissociates the productive from the privative aspect of foundational violence, the "that so often accompany" re-associates the two, reminding us that most foundational acts do not occur on blank pages of history. What was there before must be cleared away if the new authority is to *be* authoritative. Hegel's world-historical hero, destroying an old order to give birth to a new one, would be the perfect emblem of the value ambiguity of political foundings, were that hero not also portrayed by Hegel as the unwitting instrument of an upward-moving historical process.

Putting aside, for the moment, the question of whether or not it secretly serves some higher teleology, a double violence thus can be said to occur whenever one authoritative law supplants another. There is the violence of the groundlessness in right of the new right, and there is the violence of the erasure of the pre-existing right, or, more broadly, the erasure of a way of life structured and animated by that right. A continuum of foundational erasure runs all the way from the demotion of the prior right and its subordination to the higher right of the new authority, through the displacement of the prior right and the banishment of the people living under it to some space outside the new authority's domain, to the obliteration of the prior order of things along with the forcible assimilation or extermination of the people who had been attached to it. Foundational erasures along this continuum occur, for example, when a new order centralizes power over a previously helter-skelter socio-political landscape, as in the case of the emergence of the modern sovereign state form; when a new order includes some segments of the older order's population but excludes other segments, as in the cases of partitioned and ethnonational states; with radical regime change, as in the case of the shift from democracy to autocracy or vice versa; or when states impose on everyone already under their authority a shatteringly new way of life, as with state projects of modernization, collectivization, or privatization. But erasure is perhaps most traumatic when the "law of sons," to use Raskolnikov's image, replaces the law of someone else's father, as in the case of modern colonialism and settler states.

Derrida remarks that states justify their groundless authority retro-actively, by generating "proper interpretative models ... to give sense, necessity and above all legitimacy to the violence that has produced, among others, the interpretative models in question, that is, the discourse of its self-legitimation."[8] We can extrapolate the additional tendency of every state to erase from social memory the order of things it materially erased, as well as the fact that it erased it. Alternatively, every state will try to justify that material erasure by devaluing the prior order according to the new order's schema of values. These memory obliterations and justifications can be viewed as symbolic violence in the service of foundational violence. Modern instances of such symbolic violence include, sometimes singularly and sometimes in different combinations: forward-looking, progressivist contentions that a succession of peoples, modes of production, or cultures must "go under" so that humanity can advance; backward-looking, primordialist notions of the exclusive sovereign right of the first ethnic occupant to a territory long since inhabited by an ethnically mixed population; claims of the emptiness of territory before the arrival of the new authority; the association of a new regime with the will of God, and the previous regime with heresy or sacrilege; the claim of a new state to emancipate its people, and its identification of their freedom with freedom per se, so that the price other people are forced to pay for that freedom loses all significance; or a state's insistence that its overhaul of society will so enhance the wellbeing of its own population that no price *they* pay can be too high. But ultimately the very material absence of what once was present is more effective than any ideological ploy in reconciling a population to the destruction that brought a new order into being, as long as that new order has successfully forged new identities for its members in the meantime and provided them with compensatory benefits. Who can recall, in any event, a world that has long since disappeared, the longer ago it *has* disappeared, except perhaps those for whom that disappearance is so catastrophic that they or their descendants are unwilling or unable to forget, leaving them suspended over a chasm between the longed-for then and an alien now?

The American exception

Nowhere in the Western canon of political thought is foundational violence on more abundant descriptive display than in Machiavelli's

The Prince. Yet to twenty-first-century readers, the cruelties of pre-early sixteenth-century emperors, popes, kings, counts, and dukes as they vie with one another to found new political regimes seem almost quaint. The wiping out of the families of prior rulers, the despoiling of the land of those rulers' subjects, the display of butchered corpses after an invasion or annexation—these warring bids for political rule by ambitious men with distinctive personalities are light years away from the sophisticated and often abstract mechanisms by which state apparatuses with the capacity to disseminate elaborate ideologies fend off challenges to their authority or extend their power over new territory today. On the other side of the ruler/ruled equation, in contrast with the participation of the masses in the birth of so many modern states, "the people" in *The Prince* largely play the part of passive bystanders hoping to avoid oppression. While they may suffer collateral damage from the struggles between actual and would-be rulers, and while Machiavelli advises would-be rulers to seek their favor and actual rulers to secure their loyalty, the people are more an audience to the drama of politics in *The Prince* than its star actors.

The people *are* actors in the day-to-day life of republican city-states that Machiavelli describes in *The Discourses* as opposed to *The Prince*, although they must share the stage with various elites. *The Discourses* indeed articulates the republican principle of the self-government of citizens that modern democracies later will endorse and embellish in their own ways. Nevertheless, it is not until the French and American revolutions of the eighteenth century that the broad swath of "the people," or at least representatives acting in their name and purportedly on their behalf, appear in the role of founders of new sovereign state institutions and, in the American case, as founders of an entirely new sovereign state. Because of the mass character of its violence, its aim of social as well as political emancipation, and the national scale of the regime it seeks to found, the French Revolution has an impact surpassing anything that Machiavelli's princely founders *or* people could or would dream of effecting. The Revolution produces fratricidal cleavages between popular classes and hereditary elites; assaults older values and customs of rank, patronage, deference, precedence, honor, majesty, pomp, and piety; and erects a new, politically equal sovereign people where there were ladders of masters and servants before. Its destruction of traditional political institutions to clear the way for ones based on universal ideas of reason, justice, and natural right makes the French Revolution not only internally explosive but also a model of violent democratization elsewhere, whether positive (as in the eyes of the future Russian and Chinese revolutionaries who would emulate it) or negative (as in the eyes of Edmund Burke and other conservatives and reactionaries at the time).

In comparison with the French Revolution, no less than with all the imperial, monarchical, and princely conquests of earlier epochs, the United States has stood out to admirers as the great exception to the rule of political birth-by-violence, even as it stood with its French counterpart in repudiating the only other known model of state formation: the gradual, organic metamorphosis of modern political organizations and institutions out of older traditions of rule. Although these admirers do not deny that blood was spilled in its revolutionary war against the colonial despotism of Great Britain, they tout United States for founding a different way of founding political societies, offering a new archetype of political beginnings to the rest of the world.

To get a sense of how and why the United States is thus touted, let us return to Hannah Arendt, who is a more circumspect and hence a more trustworthy exceptionalist than most. As a German Jewish émigré, Arendt does not suffer from parochial blindness to the virtues of old Europe or harbor the chauvinistic prejudices of the native-born citizen. Instead of insisting that the United States has remained the freest country in the world, she confines her praise of the country to its moment of founding, before it succumbs to commercialism, bourgeois individualism, and the pursuit of infinite wealth. She also explicitly sets the American case against the foil of foundational violence, explaining precisely how it departs from that perilous path. But what makes Arendt of even greater interest here is her attempt to argue that the United States avoids not only the violence of other political foundings but also the vices of sovereign power. How she fails, and why she fails, even as she grasps the Americans' real achievement of designing their own government, provides a key to the crime at the founding of United States' sovereign power and the part that the exceptional attributes of that power played in the committing of that crime.

In *On Revolution*, Arendt frames the American Revolution as a refutation of the inescapability of foundational violence that Augustine, Nietzsche, Derrida, Raskolnikov, and Machiavelli all have suggested. She begins by noting that to Machiavelli and others, "a new beginning ... seemed to demand violence and violation, the repetition, as it were, of the old legendary crime (Romulus slew Remus, Cain slew Abel) at the beginning of all history," while "the task of foundation" seemed to entail "devising and imposing upon men a new authority" that had to cloak itself in some kind of extra-human absolute.[9] Although they share a belief in the "real meaning of the Roman *potestas in populo*, that power resides in the people," the French succumb to the violent imperatives of foundings, while the Americans defy them, except for what Arendt considers their justified fight against colonial domination but what Augustine surely would have seen as an act of fratricide.[10] The French revolutionaries, moved by boundless compassion and pity to liberate the people from their misery under the *ancien régime*, unleash "a stream of boundless violence" that deflects their revolution "almost from its beginning."[11] The American revolutionaries, "committed to the foundation of freedom and the establishment of lasting institutions," excise violence from politics in every way they can.[12] Arendt does not say much about how the Americans avoid the violence involved in the forging of a new people, except to note that even before they landed on the shores of the New World, instead of being shaped by some predatory outside force, the settlers began shaping *themselves* into a people through mutual compacts to combine "into a 'civil Body Politick.'"[13] She says much more about how the Americans avoid imposing an unauthorized law on that body, how they make the freedom of citizens the end of their government, and how they decommission the prerogatives of sovereign power, both monarchical *and* popular—all without acquiring the permanent thirst for violence that comes from wreaking havoc on an existing order of things.

How do the Americans avoid the unauthorized imposition of a new authority on human beings? Arendt emphasizes the "enormous difference ... between a constitution imposed by a government upon a people and the constitution by which a people constitutes its own government,"[14] but what exactly gives a people the authority to constitute a new governmental authority, especially when it does not become a people until after that constitution? Leo Strauss provides a "higher authority" answer to this question at the start of *Natural Right and History*, when he underlines the ideas of "self-evident truths" and "inalienable rights bestowed by the Creator" in the most famous line of the American Declaration of Independence: "'We hold these truths to be self-evident, that all men are created equal, that they are endowed by their Creator with certain inalienable Rights, that among these are Life, Liberty and the pursuit of Happiness.'" Remarking that the "nation dedicated to this proposition has now become, no doubt partly as a consequence of this dedication, the most powerful and prosperous of the nations of the earth," Strauss worries about what would happen were Americans to abandon the certainties on which their political society was originally built, of natural rights that transcend and supersede positive right.[15] Arendt worries instead about grounding political authority in an external absolute, which can serve to disguise the imposition of authority on "human material" by some external artist-fabricator. For her, it is not the "self-evident" and "Creator" but the "We hold" that is significant: the agreement by the many on the principles they wish to animate their new political society.[16] That agreement, arising out of a deliberative process initiated by the Declaration of Independence, proceeding through a series of representative assemblies, and culminating in the Constitution of the Union, is the real source of American power. The "very act of beginning" is the absolute; and it is the "act of foundation itself, rather than ... self-evident truth or any other transcendent, transmundane source" that eventually becomes "the fountain of authority in the new body politic."[17]

If the Americans create a new authority out of "mutual promise and common deliberation" or, in Alexander Hamilton's words, nothing but their own "'reflection and choice,'" what they choose and promise to establish is a polity in which "the 'passion for public freedom' or the 'pursuit of public happiness' would receive free play."[18] In contrast with the merely personal freedom they might have been allowed under tyranny, which deprives human beings of public but not necessarily private happiness, the American founders seek "a share in public business," participation in "the discussions, the deliberations, and the making of decisions," as well as the opportunity to win individual distinction in the public realm.[19] Arendt may be scathing about what happens as the republican notion of public freedom gradually gives way to the liberal idea of the free play of private interest or an individual sphere of non-interference, but she credits the Americans for initially creating a space for freedom properly, that is politically, understood.

Arendt also proposes that, while the Americans embrace the self-government of citizens, they grasp the identity of "sovereignty and tyranny" in "the realm of human affairs" and staunchly stand with freedom against sovereign power for that reason. But while she breaks with many other commentators in congratulating the Americans for their commitment to the "abolition of sovereignty within the body politic,"[20] she resembles many others in conflating popular sovereignty with the General Will, thereby eliding the possibility of a collective will that wills what is in the common interest but does not exert sovereign power, and the opposite possibility of a popular sovereign power that does not express itself as a General Will. The latter elision is particularly pertinent in Arendt's handling of the American case. It is the American founders' conviction that a free people is always variegated in its circumstances and opinions, and their consequent attempts to design political institutions to preclude the formation of a General Will that could rule society as a one-man monolith, that lead Arendt to deduce that they sought to decommission sovereign power not only in its monarchical but also in its republican form.

In line with her belief that "new beginnings" always refer back to already existing contexts, Arendt sees the political cultures against which the French and Americans rebelled as helping to shape their embrace or rejection of the General Will concept. The French deify the people as an absolute, believing in a General Will that "needs only to will in order to produce a law," not merely because they have read their Rousseau but also because they retain the ideal of absolute power from their experience of absolute monarchy and wish merely to shift that power from the king to the popular mass.[21] The Americans' conflict with England, where there is a Parliamentary counterweight to the monarch and "no absolute power absolved from laws," prompts them to create new institutions that check power without decreasing or destroying it, by separating power, multiplying power sources, and preventing, "as far as humanly possible, the procedures of the majority decisions from generating (*sic*) into the 'elective despotism' of majority rule."[22] The Americans' rejection of popular sovereign power in the form of the General Will, in short, reflects the lessons they had learned from centuries of English experience in constraining monarchical rule for the sake of individual liberty.

One implication of the fact that the Americans draw on English traditions of rule to create their new government (as well as on the colonists' own "hundred and fifty years of covenant-making," assemblage, and legislative experience[23]) is that they do not totally obliterate the law of the father when they authorize the law of the sons. But what also allows them to avoid such total destruction is the geographical distance they already had put between themselves and the old authority when they crossed the Atlantic Ocean. If it was "their own decision to leave the Old World behind and to venture forth into an enterprise entirely of their own" that led them to discover "the elementary grammar of political action," they were able to speak in that grammar by cutting their political ties to the Old World instead of having to turn that world upside down.[24] As for the other side of the same geographical coin—as Arendt tells the tale, when the settlers arrived in the New World, they met no pre-existing order but instead a "state of nature," an "untrod wilderness, unlimited by any boundary" and "still uncharted."[25] What they needed to erase was not a prior law but only the wilderness itself, and this is what, by settlement, compacts, and territorial expansion, they proceeded to do.

Re-reading the case for the American Constitution in *The Federalist Papers* on the heels of *On Revolution* prompts three further thoughts. First, however jaundiced the reader may be, in distinction from Arendt, about the agendas of James Madison, Alexander Hamilton, and John Jay—especially about their motives for fearing democracy and attempting to prevent the majority from overrunning propertied elites—there *is* much that is extraordinary about the American project of designing a new government based on the consent of the governed, not to speak of the sheer intelligence with which Madison, Hamilton, and Jay articulated and defended that design. Even the restrictions the founders sought to place on political rights—the exclusive male franchise, the agreement to count African slaves as property, and the complex system of representation they developed to ensure that the opinions of debtors and other common men could not coalesce into a hardened "public opinion" but would be properly filtered through the wisdom of their superiors—pointed the way to the undoing of those restrictions in the name of the abstract universality of those same rights later on. For the ills of political exclusion, that is, the natural rights philosophy buttressing the new political system had a fix, which became apparent as soon as those excluded from the body politic on the basis of their group status fought for full membership in political society as free and equal individuals.

Second, Arendt's idea of the founders' aversion to sovereign power is in key respects a pipedream. It is true that in the American system, it is difficult to figure out where sovereign power lies—fractured as that power is between the states and the federal government, and within the federal government, between the executive, legislative, and judicial branches—not to speak of the uncertainty as to whether sovereign power ultimately rests in a single arm of the government, the government as a whole, the Constitution, the framers of the

Constitution, or the people themselves.[26] It also is true that, although Arendt would not applaud the fact, the individualism of American culture is itself a decomposing force, militating against concentrated centers of public power and for the sovereign freedom of individuals. Nevertheless, the federalist supporters of the new Constitution, with Hamilton in the lead, were nothing if not sovereignty-obsessed. As much as they emphasized, for strategic reasons, their respect for the continued sovereign prerogatives of the states, it was sovereign power at the higher level of a central government that they were determined to institute. Indeed, one of the main reasons *The Federalist Papers* were penned was to build support for what Isaac Kramnick describes as "the triumph of the center over the periphery"[27]: the creation of a centralized state, with sovereign authority over the territory it ruled, and with, at its disposal, an army and navy, as well as the right to declare war, collect taxes, try crimes, coin and borrow money, regulate commerce, and make treaties, and, of course, to make, execute, and enforce the law. The founders may have wished to disperse sovereign power enough to preclude the resurgence of monarchical power and restrain popular power. But they also intended to magnify sovereign power by converting the potentially "unsocial, jealous, and alien sovereignties" of thirteen separate states with "thirteen distinct sovereign wills" into internally related parts of a single political unit.[28] Through the consolidation of that larger power force, the country would be able not only to squelch internal "commotions" and "insurrections" but also to preclude "discord, jealousy, and mutual injuries" between "neighbors" as "borderers" and secure itself from the "hostilities and improper interference of foreign nations," specifically Britain, France, and Spain.[29]

The third thought prompted by re-reading *The Federalist Papers* after *On Revolution* has more to do with what the two texts don't say than with what they do. The symbolic erasure of the American Indian presence in the New World that Arendt executes by portraying that world as an empty wilderness echoes the almost total absence of any reference, in either the 85 *Federalist Papers* or *The Constitution*, to the

Indian population and the life world that would have to be cleared away if a new order of things was to be born. Apart from a few brief allusions to Indians with respect to the regulation of trade, hostilities provoked by the states, and taxation and the apportionment of representatives,[30] symbolic violence in the service of foundational violence occurs in *The Federalist Papers* and *The Constitution* in the guise of silence. Very occasionally, this silence *almost* is jarring enough to disrupt the text, as when John Jay declares, in reference not to the native population but to the settler citizens of the thirteen confederated states, that "[t]his country and this people seem to have been made for each other ... as if it was the design of Providence" to bestow "an inheritance so proper and convenient for a band of brethren, united to each other by the strongest ties."[31] Most often the silence is absolutely dead—a blank non-acknowledgment that any human order of things would have to be dealt with if the new sovereign state were to *be* sovereign over any part of North America. But the conundrum that Madison, Hamilton, and Jay could evade on the page would have to be faced by the newborn republic in actual practice. How could sovereign domination be won over an already inhabited landmass in a way that was harmonious with liberty? That is, how could the United States exempt itself from Hobbes's generalization about sovereign power acquired through territorial conquest: that regardless of how a people rules itself, it rules other peoples and their places always as a despot?

The obliterating effects of the American Indian treaty system

However extravagant the pretension of converting the discovery of an inhabited country into conquest may appear; if the principle has been asserted in the first instance, and afterwards sustained; if a country has been acquired and held under it; if the property of the great mass of the community originates in it, it becomes the law of the land, and cannot be questioned—Chief Justice Marshall, 1823

Before we look at the mechanism by which the United States might be thought to warrant this exemption, we need to ask why the imposition of its sovereign power over "Indian Country" does not interest every scholar of the founding, not to speak of ordinary American lovers of freedom today.[32] Certainly part of the answer lies in the long-term effects of erasure itself. We mentioned earlier that, with the passage of time, it becomes increasingly difficult for members of a society to recall an older world that has long since disappeared, even when it had once been their world, or at least the world of their ancestors. How much more difficult it is to recall an older order of things associated with someone else's ancestors before one's own ancestors blotted it out.[33] The sheer absence of what was once present, in combination with its culturally alien quality, poses an almost insurmountable obstacle to the recognition of the violence characterizing the founding of a new sovereign authority by citizens living long after that violence has accomplished its purpose. In addition to the memory loss that follows spontaneously from this material absence and cultural chasm, various political ideas consign to oblivion whatever alien past the state has supplanted. Nationalist identifications help blind citizens to the sordid "pre-history" of their own states. With respect to the United States, right-to-left political ideologies also have played their parts.

Not unlike Arendt, contemporary American conservatives view the birth of the United States against the backdrop of European empire, monarchical rule, and social hierarchy, where its synonymy with the birth of freedom and democracy comes into high relief.[34] Against the real as opposed to the mythical backdrop of the "New World," which is as much its proper context, the birth of the United States would look more catastrophic, because of the devastation it brought to the indigenous North American population, and also less unique, as it was still possible as late as 1814 to say what General Harrison said (albeit for the self-serving purpose of soliciting Indian aid in the United States' war against the British), that white Americans *and* red ones "'were the only nations on earth who were really free, and governed by men of their own choice.'"[35] To be sure, the fact that most indigenous peoples of America were "distinguished by their sense of democracy and taste for equality"[36] does not count for much in comparison with their lack of interest in private property accumulation, the point of freedom and engine of civilizational progress for most American conservatives today.

If liberals are more ambivalent than conservatives about the American founding, it is not because they do not also see it as a great step forward for humanity, although they tend to interpret "progress" less in terms of a widening circle of possessive individualism than in terms of the increasing opportunities of individuals to cultivate themselves. Liberals are ambivalent instead because they see that step forward as not having been great enough, given that entire groups of people, most notably women and black slaves, were denied the benefits of full membership in the new society. That is, liberals view the problem of the founding as the exclusion of some groups from the enjoyment of rights and goods that American society offered other groups, not as the erasure by that society of a pre-existing social world. Leftists, for their part, are more skeptical than liberals about the possibility of equality in any capitalist society, and they are less squeamish about acknowledging the violence internal to the primitive accumulation of capital and the plunder of the Americas as an especially gruesome example of that violence. Nevertheless, many Marxist-inspired leftists have shared with liberals a developmentalist mindset that categorizes societies in terms of "backward" and "advanced" and so do not lament the fact that capitalism is, in the words of one American Indian who *does* lament it, "premised on the annihilation of tribalism."[37] This makes it difficult for either liberals or leftists to credit the cultural world the settlers discovered when they came to America with its own integrity and right to being, rather than seeing it as the most primitive point on the savage-to-civilization trajectory.

Apart from denying, misrecognizing, or excusing the violent origins of the United States, contemporary American conservatives, liberals, and leftists all romanticize popular sovereignty, even if they do so for different reasons and with different reservations. Such a romance creates its own special blinders, for in obliterating Indian America, "the people" were as active as their leaders, often acting in advance of their leaders by forcibly grabbing land for themselves that the federal government still designated "Indian Country." As Gordon S. Wood argues in *The Radicalism of the American Revolution*,[38] the availability of limitless land previously un-owned in the English sense, on which common people could settle for more than a century before and after the Revolution, was a key material condition of the development of American democracy, as it precluded the entrenchment in the New World of great inequalities between a large landowning elite and dependent landless masses. Although Wood does not make the deduction, and indeed refers to Native Americans in his text as rarely as do Publius and Arendt in theirs, this means that American democracy did not simply emerge on the ground from which Indians and their life world was being cleared but owed its very existence *as* a radical democracy to that clearance. Moreover, nineteenth-century immigrants to the United States whom liberals and leftists rightly see as victims of social discrimination participated in the same expansionist adventure that seventeenth-and eighteenth-century English and other Western European immigrants did, while twentieth- and twenty-first-century immigrants from all over the world have benefited from that adventure after the fact. In short, modern American democracy and even "multicultural democracy" were achieved (to the extent that they *were* achieved) on terrain wrested from another civilization that could not be said to deserve to go under, as the old European world could, for having an oppressive socio-political structure.

If the most obvious problem that American Indians represented for the settlers was the fact of their prior habitation of the continent (rather than any antagonism on their part to the political principles of freedom and democracy), the deeper problem was threefold. The Indian tribes' often "roaming" relationship to land and always needs-based relationship to labor was at odds with the settlers' productivity-oriented, privately bounded property system; their collectivist social relations were at odds with competitive individualism; and their spiritual relation to other species and the earth itself was at odds with the idea that everything is a means for human ends. Nothing could be more antithetical to the modern state's premise of sovereign control of territory or the capitalist premises of instrumentalism, utility, and possessive individualism than a cosmology that proposed that "all entities of nature were interrelated and that this relationship must be honored," that place "was a living presence," that the landscape was "sacred, creative, nurturing, and in motion,"[39] and that the attachment to a homeland and the enjoyment of its fruits were not entitlements to treat the land as a mere thing or to use it as a private commodity. The infamous anti-Indian racism of the Anglo-American settlers and other immigrants was, one suspects, as much the psychological effect of their inchoate understanding of the clash of mutually exclusive modes of life and their determination to crush the opposing mode in pursuit of their own interests as it was a Western hatred and fear of the other, a perverse symptom of repressed Christian sexuality, or an uncaused first cause of settler cruelty.[40] Those settler interests, in turn, were not confined to obtaining political self-governance, which was not in itself a zero-sum value. Settler interests also and more significantly turned on obtaining private ownership in land, which *was* a zero-sum value both on the individual level, given that one person's ownership of a plot of land ruled out another person's use of that same plot, and on the collective level, given that a private property system of land use ruled out different orientations to gaining sustenance from the earth. Moreover, the economic benefits the settlers sought to gain from private property whetted their appetites for more of it, as those benefits increasingly included not mere physical self-sufficiency but the profits to be made from the production of a surplus for distant markets and the enlarged capacities for consumption that such profits and markets underwrote.

It is not my purpose here to pit the virtues of a vanquished sensibility against the vices of a voracious sensibility that triumphed over it and remade the material landscape to suit its needs. Instead, I want to highlight how, between 1778 and 1871, the approximately

367 treaties signed by American Indians and ratified by the United States government were quintessential instruments of foundational violence by which Indian Territory was turned into U.S. territory and Indian Country was transformed into settler property. This is emphatically not to say that the European confrontation with the New World was not characterized by the direct physical violence of conquest, enslavement, labor exploitation, warfare, murder, and introduced disease, decimating somewhere between 75 million and 145 million indigenous people, between 8 million and 18 million of them in the area north of Mexico.[41] It is not to say that Anglo-American settlers shied away from the use of brutal force in their desire for Indian land, even while they did not manage to slaughter Indians in the mind-boggling numbers that the Spanish and Portuguese conquerors did in their search for silver and gold. It also is not to say that Anglo-American jurists were incapable of believing that "'[c]onquest gives a title which the Courts of the conqueror cannot deny.'"[42] It *is* to say that the new U.S. federal government relied centrally on agreements between reciprocally recognized sovereign nations signed in "peace and friendship" to keep shifting westward the line dividing Indian Country from settler country until that line (as the result of more forcible strategies as well) reached the Pacific Ocean. Links between popular sovereign freedom and the foundational violence of erasure, which are difficult for contemporary Americans to see because of the success of that erasure, are difficult to miss not just between the lines but also on the lines of those recorded agreements.

Those who have never had the dubious pleasure of reading through the hundreds of U.S.-American Indian treaties can be assured that, despite their individual complexities, most reveal the same core pattern.[43] Certainly, the tribes had conducted diplomatic relations through making treaties with one another, with European countries, with the colonies, and with the Continental Congress that did not exhibit the extreme asymmetry of the treaties the tribes signed with the federal government from the 1790s through 1871.[44] Many of the early treaty rituals to do with the promise of peace and friendship were indeed Indian in origin. Certainly, too, there are innumerable differences among the treaties signed by the government and Indian tribes to do with dates, tribal identities, geographical region, the particular circumstances leading up to the treaty, and the U.S. interest or lack of it, depending on those circumstances, in gaining Indian help against other European powers; acquiring a right of way through Indian lands; protecting Indians' hunting and fishing rights from the incursions of the states or individual settlers; exchanging hostages and stolen animals; establishing reservations; and inducing Indians to live in settled agrarian communities, learn the mechanical arts, and embrace private property ownership. But the most significant difference among those treaties— the exact location of the line dividing Indian from U.S. territory—also indicates their most significant constant feature: the forfeiture by Indian tribes of land they had inhabited to the United States government in return for perpetual peace, a payment of money or goods to compensate for land losses, and the promise, soon to be broken by the next treaty, that they would be forever secure in a territory to which they would be removed according to the current treaty's terms.

As Dorothy V. Jones aptly notes, the treaty system was "the primary vehicle of transfer" of land from the Indians to the United States from 1796 to 1871. But why did the "substance of dispossession" take "the form of diplomacy"?[45] Why were treaties preferred by the United States to brute violence as the means of territorial expropriation and re-appropriation? Historians allude to the specter of Indian resentment at tyranny and conquest as part of the answer, as well as the interest of the federal government in treating Indian tribes as sovereign nations to assert its prerogative of dealing with them in its tug of war for power with the states. But historians also emphasize the contradiction between violent conquest and the United States' image of itself as the champion of freedom and enemy of oppression everywhere, which required it to take land from its Indian occupants by either a just war or their consent.[46] In turn, for Indians to be considered as giving their consent, two foreground conditions had to apply, even while the threat of overwhelming physical force if they did not consent was the background condition of almost every agreement (as Thomas Jefferson put it, in his letter to William Henry Harrison in 1803, " 'We presume that our strength and their weakness is now so visible that they must see we have only to shut our hand to crush them' "[47]). First, Indians had to be recognized as enjoying sovereign agency over themselves and their territory, for otherwise they could not freely agree to cede that territory or be held responsible for sticking to their agreements.[48] Second, they had to be given something in exchange for the territory they agreed to give up, for what free agent would consent to give up something for nothing?[49]

In sum, the recognition of Indian tribes as sovereign nations enabled the United States to extend its foundational power over Indian Territory without detriment to its republican self-image, or at least with less detriment than the use of physical violence alone would have caused. Far from confirming the Indian right to self-determination, the government's recognition of Indian tribes as sovereign subjects was the necessary condition of their dispossession by consent.[50] Moreover, sovereign power in the sense of authoritative mastery and command over a bounded territory and all humans and other species within it was a European, not Indian, idea. As important as it was, given the alternatives, for Indian tribes to be recognized by the United States as sovereign nations, their incorporation within the language of sovereign power thus arguably meant they had already lost one key battle for cultural self-definition before they lost the battle for their own lands.[51] The worst irony is that the treaty system was formally suspended when Indians were judged by whites to have "lost the attributes of sovereignty"[52] as the result of all the treaties in which Indian tribes were forced, as sovereign signatories, to give up the territory on which they once were able to live as they chose.

The Anglo-American treaty system serves as a cautionary tale that familiar practices of liberty applauded by contemporary Western democracies—the deliberation between conflicting viewpoints, consensual compacts, promises of peace and friendship, and the reciprocal recognition of the sovereign independence of the deliberating, consenting, and peace-making parties—are sometimes not the counter to violence but the form that violence takes. A number of lessons can be taken away from this tale.

Most obviously, not just the creation of a new law but also the erasure of an old one need not occur solely through physically violent mechanisms. Foundational violence, which has to do with the explosive charge involved in the birth of a new order, fundamentally differs from structural violence, which has to do with ongoing asymmetrical relationships built into an established order of things. Yet the erasures characteristic of foundational violence no less than the exploitations characteristic of structural violence may be invisible *as* violence to the naked eye. The reciprocal recognition of the sovereign agency of unequal parties, for example, can be a strategy of choice by which the viability of the weaker party is assaulted by the stronger party, for to be recognized as a sovereign subject is also to be recognized as a subject who can consent to the forfeiture of the conditions necessary for the continuation of its desired way of life. The weaker party's consent to such forfeiture can be won by the stronger party's tacit threat of physical coercion if consent is withheld, even if little direct violence actually occurs.

The second lesson is that democratic sovereign states are no less likely to rest on foundational erasures than monarchical states, as nothing in the most democratic idea of "a people" prohibits its members from seeking to obliterate a prior reality incompatible with their dreams and desires.[53] What *may* distinguish, if not all democracies, at least republican and liberal ones, is their special attraction to mechanisms of violence that do not take the form of physical coercion, as well as their special interest in preserving their reputations by obliterating the memory of whatever physical violence they did commit.

The third lesson is that foundational violence in both the negative sense of erasure and the positive sense of the imposition of a new law is not limited to the period preceding the birth of a sovereign state. The crystallization of a new socio-political reality and the blanketing of its authority over a widening area can, as we have seen in the American case, take more than a century. By implication, the erasures of foundational violence can continue long after the new order institutes whatever forms of violence also are necessary for its day-to-day perpetuation, whether those forms are directly violent, as in punishment for law-breakers, or structurally violent, as in the production of class inequalities. Furthermore, erasures from the collective memory of the society of its original, material erasures can be repeated indefinitely, in annual rituals such as Columbus Day. Foundational violence in this secondary shadow sense thus may be coterminous with the life span of every state.

The fourth lesson concerns the similarities and differences between the territorial expansion of a modern sovereign nation-state and classic imperial expansion. Both forms of expansion entail foundational violence in the sense of the displacement of a prior law and the imposition of a new one over larger and larger geographical areas, but the degree of erasure they typically involve, and the project served by that erasure, differ in important respects. Classic imperial expansion characteristically results in the binding of new peripheries to a center to which they must both subordinate their will and pay tribute, but in distinction from which they are allowed to preserve something of their own character and even may enjoy semi-autonomy. The preservation of the cultural difference between imperial peripheries and centers, and their differential treatment under imperial law, indeed serves the function of marking the unequal parties who are locked together in asymmetrical power relationships. In contrast, modern nation-states typically seek to subject everyone inside their territories to the same law as members of the same people. Whether through the assimilation of minorities to the majority culture or through their expulsion or extermination, the expansion of nation-states typically involves the obliteration, over larger and larger geographical areas, of all alien authorities, languages, and ways of life. In short, imperial peoples gain from asymmetrical relations with their peripheries and the preservation of differences between center and periphery, while national peoples gain from destroying all competing orders of things and replacing them with their own.

Finally, foundational violence comes in different degrees of severity, and specific foundings therefore can be judged to be more or less cruel. Certainly: 1) the more direct violence is involved in a case of foundational violence, the crueler that violence can be said to be. However, that violence also can be said to be crueler; 2) the more radically it erases, whether via direct violence or not, a life world to which at least a group of its inhabitants was deeply attached; and/or 3) the more that erasure is imposed on an existing social reality from the outside, instead of expressing new aspirations of the existing population that the old order refused to satisfy. Outside erasures are most likely to involve the crushing of a valued past and to precipitate a politics of loss. In contrast, erasures that erupt out of the unfulfilled aspirations of an existing population remind us that there may be good reasons to endorse the foundational violence involved in the birth of a new order of things, especially if the old order was directly or structurally violent towards some or all segments of its own population. But while the future struggling to be born may be more attuned than the past to the long-stifled wishes of that population, the future that is actually born is another matter. This raises a conundrum about foundational erasures in general. Once the future has become the present, how can one determine its value relative to a past that was erased without relying on the yardstick of the victor?

Indigenous counter-sovereignty

[T]he ownership of territory is a marriage of the Chief and the land. Each Chief has an ancestor who encountered and acknowledged the life of the land. From such encounters came power. The land, the plants, the animals and the people all have spirit—they all must be shown respect. That is the basis of our law—Gitxsan People

Although, or because, the purpose of this chapter is to illustrate the interplay between freedom and domination in the birth of a sovereign United States, we would be remiss not to remark on that interplay in Native American struggles against that state.

Like indigenous peoples *vis-à-vis* settler states elsewhere, Native Americans at their most militant have challenged the authority of the United States by invoking their own status as sovereign nations. Central truths are embedded in these counter-sovereignty claims. First, Indian tribes were self-governing before the English arrived in North America, and they resisted the forfeiture of their independence by such means as raids, warfare, alliances with European enemies of the United States, and tribal confederacies to try to halt settler incursions on the continent, as well as by agreements to move to beyond the expanding borders of settler territory so that they could live as they wished. Second, although the treaties signed by Indian tribes as sovereign nations were a major vehicle of their dispossession, those treaties' recorded recognition of indigenous sovereignty, hunting and fishing rights, resource rights, rights to sacred sites, and so on have provided a strategic legal mechanism by which tribes in the contemporary period can attempt to claw back a modicum of control over the material conditions they need to sustain themselves. Third, the inclusion in American political society of tribal members either as individuals equal with all other individuals or as collective groups with minority rights equal to the rights of other minorities would not be sufficient to redeem their historical situation. The insistence of native peoples on their sovereign nationhood has always implied a repudiation of the legitimacy of settler rule over them, not a demand to be included as equals under that rule.

Nevertheless, the struggle for indigenous sovereign freedom also *belies* important truths, even while those truths are, paradoxically, well known to participants in that struggle. The most unfortunate truths have to do with material realities that militate against indigenous sovereignty. The most promising truths concern the contradiction between Western notions of sovereign power and key traditional indigenous values.

The material reality that vexes many proponents of indigenous sovereignty today is the fact that every claim to lands and resources guaranteed by past treaties must be made to the state whose sovereign authority the tribes are contesting. Thus, while native peoples did not originally consent to be governed by the United States, and while some of them may continue to see their relations with the United States as relations between distinct nations, they are forced to acknowledge the sovereign law of the U.S. government in order to gain legal recognition and protection of their treaty rights.[54] Even when its judgments happen to favor tribal interests, the settler state enjoys the higher authority to judge all legal cases within what it considers to be its borders—higher not because its moral power is superior to the moral power of the Indian nations (although that is what it claims), but because its coercive power to enforce its will is superior.

An even more irremediable factor militating against the material reality of indigenous sovereign power than the coercive power of the modern state is the destruction of the environmental pre-conditions for indigenous peoples to live according to their own lights by more than four centuries of the development of the settlers' way of life. William Cronon's study of the drastic impact of the early English settlers on the ecology of New England illustrates how the continent long ago was physically remade in ways inimical to tribal cultures. Indians' patterns of interaction with the land had allowed them to live "richly by wanting little," but "Indians could not live as Indians had lived unless the land was owned as Indians owned it." The settlers conceived of property as the exclusive control of land as a private and improvable commodity.[55] "[W]anting much," they cut down forests, fenced in fields, eroded the soil through monoculture, built roads, depleted the supply of wild animals through their appetite for furs, and so transformed the landscape that "the Indians' earlier way of interacting with their environment became impossible."[56] The colonial demolition of the material conditions for the continued flourishing of the Indian life world, with its shattering social and psychological effects, has long since been overlaid by the more pervasive and far-reaching effects of modern capitalist development, from which no one on earth can remain insulated. The sovereign power of indigenous peoples over their environment is thus fantastical both as an upshot of the native/colonial encounter and as a result of a capitalist dynamic that makes fantastical the sovereignty of all peoples across the globe.

Given the power of the law of the settler state over tribal right, and given the ecological impact of colonial ways of life on indigenous cultures and of global capitalism on everyone everywhere, the recognition of the right to sovereignty of indigenous peoples by settler states has a highly ambiguous significance. On the positive side, that recognition can serve the efforts of tribes to enhance their autonomy in delimited geographical areas, which in turn can do much to needle and even puncture the claims to sovereign power of the state itself. On the negative side, the discursive recognition of the sovereign power of native peoples does nothing to change either the settler state's coercive power to decide the law or the economic forces unleashed by the settlers' way of life that have reshaped and now may be sealing the fate of the earth, including whichever corners of the earth are recognized by settler states as rightly indigenous. In light of these twin material realities, freedom for members of indigenous peoples—although freedom of a non-sovereign sort—rests on two pre-conditions that, while they may be difficult to fulfill, are not entirely utopian.

One condition is that members of indigenous peoples participate as equal parties in a conversation with the other members of settler states about, not how the original sin of foundational violence against native populations might be redeemed (for that redemption is impossible), but how redress might be provided for the descendants of those populations. By "equal parties" I do not mean "individuals counted equally with all other individuals," for then the opinions of indigenous minorities would be outweighed by the opinions of non-indigenous majorities, but "individual members of collective bodies with equal weight in the conversation." By "redress" I mean not the lesser right of indigenous peoples, subordinated to the greater right of the sovereign state, to live in shrunken and impoverished reserves, but their right to the resources they need to flourish in the contemporary context. Admittedly, a major obstacle to the successful outcome of such a conversation is the chicken-and-egg conundrum that proper material redress already would have had to be made for indigenous voices to enjoy truly equal status with "settler" voices in any exchange of opinions between them, while a persuasive notion of what constitutes proper redress can only emerge out of an exchange in which indigenous voices already enjoy equal status, and in which, moreover, indigenous interpretations of what it means to flourish are not drowned out by "settler" interpretations.[57]

The other condition of non-sovereign freedom for indigenous peoples is that they participate equally with the rest of the world's population in decisions about how to counteract the unsustainable effects on the earth of human activity. If the first condition of indigenous freedom is difficult to satisfy, this second condition is a hundredfold more difficult, as it means that the rest of the world's population would *also* have to be able to participate in making those decisions, instead of continuing to be at the mercy of the "impersonal law of the market," the practices of private concentrations of economic power, and the "monarchical" power of modern or modernizing states. This second condition is also more urgent to satisfy, not only because the future of indigenous peoples ultimately depends on the fate of the earth, but also because global deliberations on that fate will have the greatest chance of promoting ecological wellbeing for everyone if the perspectives of indigenous peoples are central to them. The inclusion of those perspectives is vital not simply for the sake of enhancing the "democratic process" or "respecting difference" but also for substantive reasons, because of particular lines of thought and structures of feeling those perspectives traditionally have contained.

The Hegelian dialectic of the movement of every subject in its relationship to the object world from immediate unity to separation and alienation to higher unity has long since been discredited for its teleological presumptions. Nevertheless, there is something evocative of this dialectic in the potentiality of traditional indigenous value-schemes to help animate a new human relationship with the rest of the earth that is life-sustaining instead of life-destructive, if only an "immediate unity" view of the relationship between subjects and objects could penetrate a global imagination captive to the "separation and alienation stage," in order to prompt a "new and higher synthesis." This brings us to the promising conceptual truths that are obscured by the struggle for indigenous counter-sovereignty. For, while the language of sovereign freedom was embraced by Indian tribes as a counter to the sovereign power of the settler state, and while sovereign freedom continues to be endorsed by many, although not all, proponents of indigenous rights today, traditional native philosophies of life are in fundamental respects at odds with sovereign power as the Western tradition understands the term. It is precisely in the respects in which they are at odds that native philosophies offer the human species essential elements of a way to re-orient itself to the world that would help the world survive—and indeed even thrive, if not according to the yardstick currently in place.

Before we turn to the anti-sovereign intimations of indigenous philosophies, we must take a detour to see why the struggle for counter-sovereign power is nonetheless not only understandable but also almost unavoidable for any people dominated by a foreign sovereign state. Sovereign power is self-naturalizing and self-multi-plying in the sense that it often incites desires for sovereign power in those it oppresses, even when they did not have such desires before, for the simple reason that their most evident chance for freedom lies in producing a counter-concentration of power of such a magnitude that they can defeat the concentrated power of their opponent. The Native American who most famously grasped this truth was the late eighteenth/early nineteenth-century Shawnee chief Tecumseh, once he had given up on the possibility of peaceful coexistence between auton-omous Indian and settler societies. While Tecumseh followed in the footsteps of previous Indians who had struggled to build "multi-tribal alliances and pan-Indian consciousness" against settler incursions, he was unsurpassed in his passionate agitation for unity among Shawnees, Chickasaws, Choctaws, Cherokees, Creeks, Osages, the Six Iroquois

Nations, Delawares, Menominees, Kickapoos, Winnebagos, Sacs, and a host of other tribes— as well as in his formidable leadership as a warrior in the fight for pan-Indian land sovereignty on a national scale "from the Great Lakes to the Gulf of Mexico." There was an obvious paradox, however, to Tecumseh's realization that only by forming a "mighty Indian confederation" would Indian tribes have a prayer of halting the expansion of United States power and authority for good.[58] The tribes had relatively small numbers of members, heterogeneous proclivities and practices, often "mutually unintelligible" languages, and separate heads or chiefs, who, not possessing sovereign prerogatives, relied on "persuasion, example, and consensus"[59] to sway others. If those tribes could avoid defeat at the hands of a centralized sovereign power only by combining under the central command of a single leader, they would ultimately forfeit those same attributes to what would have to become, whether Tecumseh envisioned it or not, a permanent counter-sovereign power in order to stave off all future foreign sovereign state assaults. Two practical generalizations can be deduced from this paradox. On the one hand, as tribes too jealous of their independence to unite under Tecumseh soon discovered, once a sovereign power arises, and as long as it is vigorous, only counter-sovereign power can curtail or annihilate its force. On the other hand, as those tribes intuitively knew, the autonomy and self-rule of communities will suffer once counter-sovereign power is amassed on their behalf.

A conceptual generalization follows from these practical ones. Autonomy, self-rule, and sovereignty are often treated today as synonyms by Western and indigenous thinkers alike. While all these concepts overlap, autonomy and self-rule are not identical with sovereign power and should be teased apart from it. "Autonomy" suggests the ability to live independently, according to one's own dispositions, habits, desires, values, and preferences. "Self-rule" suggests the ability to decide on the principles and norms that will govern one's actions and to act according to them. Such dispositions, values, principles, and norms need not accord with the sovereignty principle. Indeed, autonomy and self-rule in and of themselves entail the absence of any outside master, and neither autonomy nor self-rule entails an inside master in the sense of a self that controls itself and its surroundings—although "self-rule" *may* involve self-mastery if the self's norms for action are rigid and hostile to its own spontaneous inclinations, and "autonomy" *may* involve other-mastery if the self's distinction between itself and its surroundings is so sharply drawn as to require fortification against everything outside that line. In contrast, "sovereignty," as we have seen earlier, signals the *presence* of a master: in its classic monarchical form, as a commanding power that makes and imposes the law on a subject population; in its popular sovereignty form, as a commanding power that makes and imposes the law on itself as a distinct people; in either case, as a power that controls everything beneath it inside a bounded space; and, if sovereignty is seen as the path to freedom, as a power that is driven to try to control everything outside that space that otherwise might impinge on it.[60]

Notwithstanding the fact that indigenous struggles often have been couched as struggles for sovereignty, how have indigenous value-schemas in North America and elsewhere clashed with the sovereign power ideal?

William Cronon gives us the key to part of the answer when he describes the habits of mobility on which "[a]ll aspects of Indian life [in early New England] hinged"[61]; their conception of property in terms of usufruct rights, so that different tribes or peoples could have different claims on the bounty of the same land or water mass in different seasons; and their practices of interacting with the environment to preserve the maximum of abundance and diversity of species with the minimum of work. While the English at the time justified their expropriation and enclosure of the land by the Indians' failure to subdue and improve the soil, at our end of the "subdue and improve" trajectory we call progress, we can only marvel at those Indians' light ecological footprint, their "relative indifference to property accumulation," their appreciation of the earth as an "ecological cornucopia," their generosity in sharing that cornucopia with early settlers, and their combination of the sense of the sacredness of their homelands with an allergy to the excluding function of physical boundaries.[62]

If the early North American Indian relationship to the land is at odds with the idea of sovereign power over a fixed territory, so is the traditional North American Indian penchant for community self-rule by consensus as opposed to rule by a centralized state differentiated from society. Underpinning both economic and political attitudes are philosophical principles to which the rubric of sovereign power does a categorical injustice. Taiaiake Alfred sums up these principles as the belief in "responsibility to all creation" as the highest value (at odds with the idea of the sovereign master as the highest value); the commitment to "respectful, balanced co-existence among all human, animal, and spirit beings, together with the earth" (at odds with the imperative to master others), and a conception of justice as the "restoration of harmony to the network of relationships," not only among human beings but between human beings and all the other creatures and natural elements of the universe, in a way that demonstrates "true respect for the power and dignity of each part of the circle of interdependency" (at odds with the idea of separate selves for whom justice centers on claiming rights, including sovereignty rights, against other selves and species).[63]

After noting that "the suitability of sovereignty as the primary political goal of indigenous people has gone largely unquestioned," Alfred condemns not only the "intense possessive materialism at the heart of Western economies" but also the "acceptance of sovereignty as the framework for politics today," which "reflects the triumph of a particular set of [social, not natural] ideas over others."[64] He rejects the concept both for its "exclusionary" portrait of politics as a "zero-sum contest for power" and for its irrelevance to indigenous communities, where there is "no absolute authority, no coercive enforcement of decisions, no hierarchy, and no separate ruling entity."[65] As for relations between indigenous and settler nations—he avoids endorsing the domination inherent in sovereign power and the solipsism inherent in sovereign freedom, hoping instead that these nations can co-exist by respecting each other's autonomy as "two vessels, each possessing its own integrity, travelling the river of time together."[66] Of course, one of those vessels first would have to make radical changes in its behavior.

The inconceivability of such changes, and the consequent threat to the other vessel, is probably one reason why many indigenous thinkers would agree with Dale Turner that indigenous rights to sovereignty must be defended.[67] Yet Turner acknowledges that colonialism has left its stamp on "the very ways that we frame the language of rights, sovereignty, and nationalism,"[68] and he describes indigenous philosophical principles in terms identical with Alfred's. These terms can be seen in a passage Turner highlights from the political philosophy of the Gitxsan people, which I borrowed for the epigraph of this section of this chapter. Turner may be strategically astute to present these lines as evidence for an Aboriginal concept of sovereignty against the claims to sovereign power over Aboriginal peoples of, in Turner's case, the Canadian state. However, Alfred is philosophically wiser in seeing respect for "the land, the plants, the animals and the people" as expressive of a sensibility to which the desire for sovereign power is alien.

Social and natural exterminations

In *The Conquest of Nature: Water, Landscape, and The Making of Modern Germany*, David Blackbourn recalls an analogy drawn by Nazi leaders between what anyone else would have seen as diametrically opposed political societies: the federal republic of the United States of America and totalitarian Germany. The analogy had nothing to do with the internal political institutions of the two nations, and everything to do with their approach to the world they confronted at the landed edge of their sovereign borders. While full of scorn for the decadence of the United States in their own period, Nazi leaders praised the indomitable frontier spirit of early American settlers in their east-to-west battle against the wilderness, taking special note of the ruination of American Indians as a consequence of that process. Indians were, to be sure, noble savages in the Nazis' rendition of the tale.[69] Still, according to the Nazis, the Indians were doomed to perish in light of the civilizational superiority of European immigrants, and the unruly qualities of the land through which the Indians wandered as nomads, not masters, were also fated to disappear. To acquire greater living space as well as to become toughened through the fortifying rigors of frontier experience, the Germans now had to wage their own wilderness battle, this time west-to-east, into Bohemia-Moravia, Greater Poland, and Ukraine. Degenerate Jews and indolent Slavs, whom the Nazis called their own "redskins," would have to be displaced so that vast wetlands, steppes, and wastelands could be properly reclaimed. It first was hoped that the offending races would perish by attrition through being forced to labor under sub-human conditions in the least habitable eastern areas of the land marked for future German settlement. Soon, however, events depriving them of the leisure of taming their wilderness over many decades, the Nazis decided to drain at least their "human swamps" as quickly as possible by deporting their inhabitants to mass killing centers.[70]

Blackbourn presents as tightly interlinked the projects of cleaning out "inferior" peoples and cleaning up an "unkempt" countryside to suit a mixture of aesthetic, industrial, military, and even ecological aims. In the short run, the extermination of peoples succeeded, while the extermination of vaporous marshes and unhealthy moors never came to full fruition. In the long run, however, the social extermination project proved a failure, as Jews and Slavs, unlike their indigenous Americans counterparts, rebounded from the loss of millions of their numbers. In contrast, the natural extermination project has continued unabated. But while they rightly could be charged with crimes against humanity, it would be impossible to pin ongoing crimes against nature, if we are willing to call them crimes, on Nazi leaders and their legacy alone. After all, almost every state in the modern world that enjoys or aspires to "greatness"—regardless of whether it has been politically fascist or liberal, or has taken a capitalist or communist path to economic growth, or applauds (as the Nazis did) or denigrates ideals of nature conservation—has exploited nature for its own purposes without making more than minor ameliorating efforts. Private corporations have shared center stage with states in this venture and even can be said to have stolen the limelight from them, but mass sentiments also have played an inciting role. In 1930s and 1940s Germany, those sentiments might have been traceable to delusions of grandeur on the part of a so-called master race. In the contemporary global context, popular enthusiasms for the conquest of nature partly reflect hopes for greater national prowess and stature on the part of citizens of particular countries. More importantly, however, those enthusiasms reflect desires for material wellbeing, as that term is generally interpreted today, on the part of individuals as simple members of the human race. Thus, while many in our age continue to feel horror at Germany's descent into genocidal politics, far fewer would find much to condemn in a passage Blackbourn quotes from a 1942 article in the SS journal, *The Black Corps*: "'[W]e have diverted rivers, built highly fruitful polders below the surface of the sea, drained marshes and moors ... until we have given the landscape a human imprint, our own countenance.'"[71]

Let us return briefly to Hannah Arendt, who once again exemplifies, with greater subtlety and refinement than others, a more general problematic stance. This time the stance involves a split between what we might call a critical social and natural consciousness. Although the split can work in the opposite direction, in Arendt's case it takes the form of an acute sensitivity to the extermination of peoples that arises out of the historical dynamic of socio-political affairs, and a lack of attunement to the natural world that is susceptible to the same fate as a result of that dynamic.

Thus, on the one hand, even as she evades, in *On Revolution*, the impact on Indians of Anglo-American settlement, Arendt works assiduously to untangle, in *The Origins of Totalitarianism*, the threads that run from European overseas imperialism, with its exterminist binges against colonized populations, to European continental imperialism, with its climax in the Holocaust. While she sees the capitalist search for infinite profit as key to overseas imperialism and pan-movement fantasies of ethnonational supremacy as key to continental imperialism, the notion that whole peoples are at best exploitable and at worst extinguishable is to her mind the pernicious core of the two cases. Moreover, she suggests that it was because, in the former case of imperialism, one race had used its power to subjugate or massacre another almost without thinking, that in the latter case racial massacre could be readily imagined and methodically carried out.

On the other hand, Arendt is notoriously tone-deaf to natural species, landscapes, and biological life cycles as either providing valuable pleasures in human life or as being distinctive values in themselves. The signature of civilization is indeed for her, if not the literal extermination of nature, then its transformation in accordance with higher human values. To be sure, with respect to, not what William Cronon calls the "first nature" of the earth as its exists before human intervention, but the "second nature" of the earth as it has been materially reshaped, Arendt condemns, in *The Human Condition*, the capitalist drive for infinite wealth. By ceaselessly destroying and recon-structing the built environment, that drive denies human beings a relatively permanent set of private and public enclosures that can serve as the stable physical backdrop for ephemeral human interactions, words, and deeds. She also warns readers in that same work of the unpredictable and uncontrollable chain of events that may occur once human beings "act into nature" by instigating entirely new physical processes, and she attacks the mentality of the sovereign subject for turning everything in the world into instrumental means for its own ends. These three provisos are so important that they might be fruit-fully incorporated into any critical theory of nature and society. Given them, however, Arendt's sympathies lie decidedly with, not against, substituting for first nature a fabricated second nature to suit civiliza-tional purposes.

As Blackbourn would lead us to expect, a disdain for first nature not only has problematic environmental implications but also easily can be broadened to include peoples who live in close relation to first nature or only modestly transform it into second nature. Arendt registers the social if not the natural after-effects of that disdain in *The Origins*, when she imagines the shock Europeans must have felt on first encountering tribes in Southern Africa living in close proximity to nature without doing much to replace it with human artifacts. It is the difference between the designing attitude towards nature of the Europeans and the deferential attitude towards nature of the African tribes, she argues, rather than the difference in skin color, that explains the crystallization of the idea of how "peoples could be converted into races" and how "one might push one's own people into the position of the master race."[72] Even members of the European lower classes, by banding together with their own ruling elites under the common rubric of race, could assert the prerogatives of sovereign mastery in Africa on the basis of their membership in a culture that had learned how to civilize nature instead of living at its mercy. In short, however parasitical or criminal they might have become as a result of their efforts, first the Boers and then the European adventurers arrived at the idea that they could dominate Africans on the grounds that the latter were "different from other human beings" in "that they behaved like a part of nature, that they treated nature as their undisputed master, that they had not created a human world, a human reality, and that therefore nature had remained, in all its majesty, the only overwhelming reality."[73]

It is difficult to ignore echoes in Arendt of the same condescension towards those who fail to build a nature-obliterating material culture that she believes provided Europeans with the license for race domination in Southern Africa, even as she sharply criticizes race domination. But whether or not one shares that condescension, which is now a symptom less of Euro-centrism than of industrial- and post-industrial-society-centrism, it is indisputable that the tribal peoples who are its targets did not bring the earth to the ecological breaking point at which it has arrived in the brief time span since Westerners first arrived to settle America and plunder Africa. Nor, for that matter, was the earth brought to that brink by the practices of agrarian societies, in pre-modern Europe and pre-colonial regions elsewhere, in which the rhythms of nature determined to an important extent the limits of human self-conception, needs, and aims. Today, however, when a propensity for treating nature as a mere object to serve the multiplying desires of a sovereign subject has spread so rapidly across the globe that it threatens both subject and object with oblivion, the challenge "to de-think the concept of sovereignty,"[74] as Taiaiake Alfred puts it, takes on environmental, not just political, urgency and import. This is so even if a change in thinking is a necessary but hardly a sufficient condition of avoiding that oblivion.

Admittedly, nations and classes that have benefited the most from the conquest of nature may not feel any inclination to concur, and, indeed, the modern history of state-formation, industrialization, and capitalist development continues to pull humanity in the opposite direction. However, as we face the calamitous consequences of that conquest, not only the descendants of settler societies but also avid commodity consumers across the globe may be forced to revise their position, at least with respect to human-earth relations. Unfortunately, what will force us is a moment of great ecological crisis, which is likely to be a moment too late. Unfortunately, too, the belief that the human race must exert even greater mastery over the earth to manage the consequences of environmental crisis is meanwhile becoming a new "common sense." But while advanced scientific knowledge will have to be harnessed to temper the effects of ecological distress, science can provide only the technical aid needed to cope with this problem. To achieve the requisite metamorphosis in the self-understanding and will of the human species, philosophical as well as technical wisdom is required. And of the available shards of philosophical wisdom that are at the world's disposal, the indigenous idea of the intrinsic integrity, "spirit," and interdependence of all species and elements of the earth, which many environmentalists already embrace, may be our best fresh ontological starting point.

As for the social aspect of the environmental crisis: when ever-increasing material abundance comes up against ecological limits to growth, we will be confronted with a new version of the old "barbarism or socialism" choice. The few can enjoy vast riches in climate-controlled enclaves while the many are consigned to environmental deterioration and deprivation, or the world can pivot towards a new concept of what G. A. Cohen has called "equality for a context of scarcity."[75] Elaborating this concept in a way that provides people in diverse cultural and socio-economic situations with a promising vision of a new kind of wellbeing would take us far beyond the scope of this study. Let us simply say, in closing, that indigenous perspectives are once again pertinent here. Those perspectives offer an encouraging clue that it is possible for everyone to "live richly, by wanting little"—or at least, at this point in history, "by wanting less."

Epigraphs

Fyodor Dostoyevsky, *Crime and Punishment*, trans. Richard Pevear and Larissa Volokhonsky (New York: Vintage, 1993 [1867]), 260.

Quoted in Bryan H. Wildenthal, *Native American Sovereignty on Trial: A Handbook with Cases, Laws, and Documents* (Santa Barbara, CA: ABC-CLIO, 2003), 23. Chief Justice John Marshall is commenting in Johnson v. M'Intosh (1823).

Political philosophy of the Gitxsan people. Quoted in Dale Turner, *This is Not a Peace Pipe: Towards a Critical Indigenous Philosophy* (Toronto: University of Toronto Press, 2006), 66–7.

The Search for Sovereign Freedom

De te fabula narratur!—Karl Marx, *Capital*

The price of sovereign freedom for the other

"Sir! We're to be flogged because you complained about us to the Examining Magistrate" … said Willem, interrupting himself to clap his hand, over which he had got a stinging blow with the rod, to his mouth. "We are only being punished because you accused us … Both of us, and especially myself, have a long record of trustworthy service … we had every prospect of advancement and would certainly have been promoted to be Whippers pretty soon, like this man here."—Franz Kafka, *The Trial*

Our story of the Jewish search for sovereign freedom has a very different narrative arc from our story of the founding of the United States. That first tale recounted how erasures of the Indian life world paved the way for the English settlers to build, in Arendt's words, a new house where freedom can live, at least as those settlers understood the freedom concept. It concluded with indigenous insights on the value of non-sovereign relations of the human race to the rest of the earth. This second tale runs, chronologically if not in the order of presentation here, from the modern European oppression of the Jews to the search for Jewish sovereign freedom in Palestine to a new dialectic of mastery and servitude, with Jews in the position of the master. An unexpected truth follows from the fact that the Jewish state is built on a great crime against Palestinian Arabs but was instigated by an even greater crime against the European Jews. This is the truth that the experience of persecution can be a stony ground for the cultivation of empathy towards others who are suffering from persecution and even can be the root cause of that suffering.

Although America can be traced back to one original sin,[1] while Israel must be traced back to two, it is hard not to notice lines of resemblance between their founding processes, if one looks at those processes from the vantage point of their victims instead of their protagonists. There is the same unexpected appearance of religiously and politically inspired settlers from afar, the same multiplication over time of their numbers, and the same dawning realization of the indigenous population that the growth of settler communities represents a threat to life as it had been lived until then. There is the same obliterating myth the first settlers bring with them of an empty territory awaiting their arrival and the same self-absorbed dream to make the land, whether conceived of as a bountiful wilderness or a barren desert, productive for themselves. There is the same condescension towards the natives, obtuseness to the value of indigenous socio-cultural life as it is lived in a particular place, and inability or unwillingness to understand the true impact on others of their own activities or to empathize with them. Alternatively, on the part of settlers who *do* understand, and consequently know they will be hated by the population they hope to displace, there is the same fierce determination to win the battle between diametrically opposed collective interests.

Although the Jews who came to Palestine inserted themselves into a largely agrarian/urban instead of nomadic/agrarian society, there is also a discrepancy less severe but still evocative of the one we saw in the American case between settler and native material technologies, modes of organization, forms of knowledge, institutional structures, and political philosophies. Weirdly enough, there is even, by the 1920s, a special connection to and later a rebellion against the imperial power, Great Britain, with which the American settlers had been entangled, although the background causes of those connections and rebellions are in each case distinct. Finally, there is the same dynamic in which a nascent settler society stretches over a larger and larger swath of territory, culminating in a centralized sovereign state that creates right inside that still-expanding territory but is unauthorized to do so by any prior authority that is higher, more objective, or more universal than itself.[2]

Like their analogues in North America, the builders of the state of Israel made use of both "peaceful" and aggressive modalities of violence to transform the pre-existing world in Palestine into a new reality. If those modalities warrant exemplification here, it is only in part because, while they are like the American prototypes in gross generalities, they are unlike them in many particulars. More to the point, any consideration of the boomerang effects on the Jews of their search for sovereign freedom must begin with the directly punishing effects of that search on Palestinian Arabs, for ethical reasons and also because Palestinian responses to those effects, and Israel's responses to those responses, reveal sovereign freedom to be a pipedream for both parties, as neither is free from the impact of the other to be a master of its fate.

Much of world Jewry looks back at the struggle for a Jewish state with great romance. Both the Zionists who by the late nineteenth century had over-shadowed the mystical and orthodox Jewish minority in the Ottoman-governed Holy Land and the generation that fought to found Israel after World War II viewed their own ideals, sacrifices, and courage with romance, too. Nevertheless, the victory of the Zionist struggle hinged on one quite down-to-earth consideration, of which the early pioneers could not help but become aware once the blinding light of the idea of Jewish national regeneration had given way to a grasp of demographic realities on the ground.[3] In the perhaps apocryphal words of one Jewish visitor to Palestine, "The bride is very beautiful, but she is betrothed to another." How could the Jews win that bride, when Muslim and Christian Arabs in the years Zionists began to ask this question outnumbered Jews by at least twenty-two to one and even by the end of World War I still made up 90 percent of the population?[4]

From the 1920s on, various plans for Jewish-Arab federations and confederations were designed by Zionists of different political hues to try to square the circle for themselves, at least until they had acquired the numbers to change the basic equation in their favor, but also to show how it was possible to create an ethnic majority society that did not oppress minorities as European societies had done. These plans included everything from complete bi-national parity between Jews and Arabs in an ethnically intermixed community; to separate, ethnically autonomous cantons in a larger bi-national federation; to a Jewish state in some portion of Palestine within a larger Arab federation; to a sovereign Jewish state in all of Eretz Israel guaranteeing its Arab minority equal rights and cultural autonomy. But except in the case of perfect bi-national equality, each idea rested on two premises that made its practical success very difficult for any neutral observer to imagine, not to mention any Arab, for whom even bi-national equality was unpalatable. These premises were a general recognition of "the national right of the Jewish people to Palestine, i.e. Eretz Israel" and "a Jewish majority in Palestine."[5] In combination, such bedrock principles required the reduction of the Arab population to a minority in that same space, to be achieved by two basic mechanisms. One mechanism was increasing Jewish immigration into Palestine, and indeed, as a result of Zionist mobilization in the context of successive waves of European anti-Semitism, by 1947 immigration had boosted the Jewish proportion of the population in Palestine to one third. The other mechanism was enticing or forcing out of some large portion of Palestine as many Muslim and Christian Arabs as possible.[6] While building a Jewish majority through in-migration would have obvious political and cultural costs for Palestinian Arabs, the worst forms of foundational violence involved in the creation of Zionist settlements, the birth of the Jewish state, and the state's territorial expansion were all of the "pushing out" variety.

Before we review specifics of this "pushing out" process—specifics for which we owe critical Israeli scholars a great debt for helping to expose—we need to revisit the question of the words we use to say things about political life. What terms of political discourse best capture this particular effort to replace, in the same geographical area, what Frantz Fanon once called "a certain 'species' of men by another 'species' of men," from the point of view of the former "species"?[7] More exactly, what term best captures this effort in the absence of mass

extermination, for which vicious project, thanks to conceptual innova-
tions after Nazism, we now have the word "genocide"? Two nouns
popular with Zionism's fiercest antagonists—"imperialism" and a sui
generis "Zionist entity"—both are misleading, the second dangerously
so, although features of Zionism open it to the charge of "imperialism,"
while Jewish mythologies feed into the sui generis notion.

The association of Zionism with imperialism has more than a few
grains of truth to it. After all, Zionism was a self-conscious colonizing
project, and many Zionists exhibited typical Western attitudes of racial
and civilizational superiority over the peoples of what now is called the
Middle East, even promising European countries that a Jewish state in
Palestine could serve as an outpost of Western influence and a bulwark
between Europe and Asia. Then, too, Zionist leaders attempted to make
deals with rulers of several imperial regimes, including the Ottoman
Sultan, and came to pin most of their hopes on Great Britain's on-again,
off-again support for a Jewish state in Mandatory Palestine, embracing
its imperial power over the area until near the end. The state of Israel
has always identified itself strongly with the West, and these days,
especially with the United States, which is not unreasonably viewed
by many in the Middle East as a neo-imperial power. From the 1970s
until the mid-1990s, Israelis benefited, in typical imperialist style,
from cheap Arab labor as a result of their occupation of Gaza and the
West Bank, a reprise of the use of Arab physical labor by Jewish citrus
cultivators before Israel was born. Finally, Israel's ambition to increase
its territory, the same kind of ambition that the Americans had approv-
ingly called "imperial" when describing their own westward expansion
across North America, resembles the iconic outward spread of all
ancient and modern imperialist powers. Still, it would be a mistake
to characterize the essential impetus and raison d'être of either the
Zionist movement or the state of Israel (or, for that matter, the continental expansion of the United States) as imperialist in the strict sense
of an ongoing exploitation of asymmetries of power between a ruling
people in the core and the diverse peoples it conquers in the periphery.
Instead, exclusive self-rule in a territory large enough to sustain the

collective ethnos has always been the driving and, for Palestinian Arabs, ominous desire here.

The charge that Zionism does not fit under any category more general than itself but represents a total evil all its own is a strong implication of the second term, "the Zionist entity," when that phrase is used by Zionism's enemies. The idea of a total evil also is implied by the simple equation of Zionism with racism, as if there would be no remainder to Zionism once racism was subtracted. The idea of a total evil that is sui generis seems at times the subtext of that equation as well, as if the racism that is Zionism were a singular kind of politics or, even worse, a manifestation of something singularly Jewish. While outrage at Israeli injustices to Palestinians and classic anti-Semitism have played separate parts in fostering the idea that Zionism is unique in its abominations, two features of Jewish self-representation and political argumentation have helped the idea not of abomination but of uniqueness to take hold. As Hannah Arendt pointed out in her 1967 preface to the first volume of *The Origins of Totalitarianism*, the belief of many Jews that they are God's chosen people, and/or that they have a special mission on earth, and/or they have been eternal scapegoats victimized by everyone everywhere, suggests that the Jews are in mysterious ways separated from all other peoples, so that ordinary categories into which other human beings fall, and failings to which other human beings are susceptible, do not apply to them. While Arendt went on to pinpoint the dangers for Jews of exceptionalist self-conceptions in the nineteenth-century European setting, those self-conceptions are equally dangerous in the context of Middle Eastern politics today. Most obviously, the claim of many Jews that any criticism of Israel is anti-Semitic feeds the idea that whatever injustices Israel inflicts on Palestinians is the outer manifestation of an inner Jewish essence.

To file Zionism instead under the rubric of *ethnonationalism*, as this chapter will do, is to reinsert it in a larger universe of problematic modern politics inhabited by other individuals and peoples. Zionism does not stand alone in its vulnerability to terms used to characterize and appraise ethnonationalism, but by the same token it is not exempted by some metaphysical special status from their categorization of its human, all-too-human sins.[8]

Instead of emerging from within a mixed-belt territory that it then sought to take over, Zionism came from elsewhere to claim an already inhabited territory for another ethno-religious group. While not reducible to racism with no remainder, Zionism exhibited *racist* attitudes and practices. As noted earlier, many Western Zionists had absorbed European attitudes of civilizational superiority and reiterated those attitudes when they encountered the indigenous Palestinian population. Furthermore, to account for Arab resistance as well as the hostility of various Western state officials to their enterprise, Zionists were not above drawing on traditional notions of an essential alienation between Gentile and Jew. Most significantly, the Zionists sought to create a society in which the line between national majority and minority, and national insider and outsider, was drawn on the basis of ethno-religious "blood." In combination, these race discriminations helped set in motion two interacting antinomies: the antinomy of superior and inferior, in which the individual's assignment to majority or minority within the state was based on the fixity of being, not the shifting sands of political opinion; and the antinomy of friend and enemy, in which members of antagonistic collective identities faced one another both inside and outside the state's territorial bounds. In turn, these antinomies fuelled the combustible emotions of arrogance, resentment, pride, scorn, humiliation, indignation, hatred, and fear, which then exacerbated the antinomies, which intensified the combustible emotions in a downwardly spiraling loop.

As is true of other ethnonational movements and settler colonies alike, it can be said that Zionism acquired the territory for the Jewish state by myriad practices of *dispossession*— territory from which both the material and memory traces of dispossession were then *erased*. In its attempts to de-Arabize the land it claims for the Jewish people, the state of Israel can be accused of *ethnic cleansing*, a metaphor for which this time we have Serbian nationalists to thank. All these practices, whether "peaceful" or coercive, can be counted as modalities of *foundational violence*. That is, with every plot of land that is swept within the boundaries of the Jewish state, and every Arab who is swept out or demoted to the status of an ethnic stranger, the state extends its law over a new space for the benefit of a different population.

The earliest and most "peaceful" modality of foundational violence in the struggle for a Jewish state was the consensual contract, but not a contract in the American form of treaties signed by reciprocally recognized yet unequal sovereign nations that transferred land from the weaker to the stronger party. Instead, beginning some seven decades before Israel came into existence, private contracts of purchase and sale between Jewish pioneers financed by Jewish philanthropists abroad and large, mostly absentee Arab landowners were the instruments by which land was transferred parcel by parcel from the latter to the former. If, in the words of one Zionist in 1882, the idea " 'is, in time, to take over the Land of Israel and to restore to the Jews the political independence they have been deprived of for these two thousand years,' " as another Zionist noted later, only three modern methods of land acquisition were theoretically available: conquest, government expropriation, and private purchase. Private purchase was what the Zionists had to rely on, " 'until at some point we become rulers.' "[9] The political effects on Arab society of these early private land sales were modest, but the economic and psychological effects were marked, above all for poor Arab peasants, who before the Zionists arrived already had been reduced by circumstances of indigenous class domination to tenant farmers on land they once had owned as small proprietors and now were evicted from that land.[10] Although many were able to earn wages, even higher wages than before, as field hands for the first wave of Jewish immigrant farmers, they not only had lost to foreigners their final hold on their home on earth but also had to put up with the contemptuous treatment that colonial overlords all too often mete out to native underlings. Indeed, by 1891 the spiritual Zionist Ahad Ha-Am (who later was to warn that "a political ideal which is not grounded in our national culture" would "beget in us a tendency to find the path of glory in the attainment of material power

and political dominion"[11]) protested that the settlers were exhib-
iting towards Arab peasants " 'a tendency to despotism as happens
always when a slave turns into a master.' "[12] Ironically, the livelihood
of those peasants was more seriously threatened once a radical wave
of Jewish immigrants arrived in Palestine. Determined to re-fashion
the diasporic urban Jew into a muscular worker of the soil,[13] unable
to compete with more competent and compliant Arab agricultural
workers, and allergic on socialist grounds to the colonial exploitation
of one race by another, those left-wing immigrants endorsed the policy
and practice of Jewish-only labor.[14]

Unlike the private land contract, most forms of foundational violence
in Palestine/Israel were enabled and legitimated by wars sometimes
initiated by others, sometimes initiated by Israel, and often the result
of escalating tensions between everyone. That "everyone" included
Israeli Jews and Palestinian Arabs but also other Arab states, including
Egypt, Syria, Lebanon, Jordan, and Iraq. Some forms of foundational
violence were unplanned by-products of war, and some were orchestrated by the Zionist leadership. They most infamously included,
during the first Arab-Israeli war, the expropriation of Palestinians
who had fled the new Jewish state in a panic in 1948 in fear of Jewish
military attack and/or under advisement of near-by Arab countries; the
intimidation and forced expulsions of others from their homes, fields,
and stores; the transfer of Arabs from one part of the new country to
another for military security purposes or to make room for Jews; and
the looting and destruction of Arab villages or their repopulation with
Jewish immigrants.[15] The ultimate effect of such violence was a gain
of more than half a million acres for Jews in addition to the over 55
percent of Mandatory Palestine that the United Nations had allotted
to them and the transformation of between 600,000 and 750,000 Arab
residents of Palestine into refugees, as well as the political isolation and
military supervision of more than 100,000 Arabs who remained on
what became Israeli soil and another few thousand allowed back after
the war.[16] Administrative and military decrees such as the "Absentees
Property Law," "Law of Land Acquisition in Times of Emergency,"

and "Emergency Regulation of the Cultivation of Fallow Lands" also functioned in this period as non-directly violent instruments of foundational violence. To take the first example, property from which Arabs had fled was counted by law as the abandoned property of absentees and as such made available for new Jewish owners. Even thousands who had fled from their property for only a few days and remained inside the borders of Israel were stripped of their property after being designated as "present absentees."[17]

Many liberal and left-leaning Jews make a moral distinction between the legitimate creation of a Jewish state in 1948 and an illegitimate Occupation of the West Bank and Gaza in 1967. They also distinguish between a humanistic leadership in the pre-1967 period and an aggressively nationalistic leadership afterwards with roots in a right-wing "Revisionist" Zionism that early idealistic Zionists had reviled.[18] Nevertheless, the Sharons, Begins, Netanyahus, Liebermans, and Bennetts who successively moved to political center stage after 1977 are in the most important respect—their commitment to Jewish sovereign power in Palestine—as tightly related to the liberal Theodor Herzl and the leftist David Ben-Gurion as they are to the Revisionist Vladimir Jabotinsky and the sometimes brown-shirted Zionists who in the 1920s and 1930s took their political cues from him.[19] Inversely, despite Jabotinsky's "maximalist" position that land on both sides of the Jordan River should belong to a Jewish state, his bellicosity towards Palestinian Arabs until the day they would be forced to accept minority status in that state, his distaste for the Orient, his view of Arabs as civilizationally backward, and the Jewish left's view of him as a fascist, this Revisionist, to whom we will return later, deserves appreciation from Zionism's foes and friends alike in two connected respects.[20] First, although he had been circumspect early on, he later was more honest than other Zionists in calling outright for a Jewish sovereign state in Eretz-Israel, instead of publicly endorsing a nebulous cultural homeland for the Jews while working for Jewish political sovereignty in Palestine behind the scenes. Second, unlike the liberal and leftwing Zionists who imagined that a Jewish state in Palestine could somehow live in peace with its Arab inhabitants, Jabotinsky understood the inevitability of a clash between two peoples with awakened national aspirations and designs on the same "bride."

To trace the thread of continuity that runs from the pre-state through the post-Occupation periods, we need only consider how foundational violence in the years just before and after 1948 anticipate the modalities by which Israel, after 1967, stretched its sovereign power over more and more of Mandatory Palestine while excluding the new inhabitants it acquired from "the sovereign people."

The first key continuity between 1948 and 1967 is the creation in both periods of a Palestinian refugee population, with the effect of reducing the number of Arabs on land desired for the Jews. More specifically, the flight of those hundreds of thousands of Arabs from Palestine during the first Arab-Israeli War prefigures the flight during the Six-Day War, whether from panic or Israeli military intimidation, of between 200,000 and 250,000 Palestinians from the West Bank, along with 100,000 Arab refugees who fled from or were pushed out of the Golan Heights.[21] At the same time, however, Israel gained in the Occupation over a million new Palestinian inhabitants, a number reaching almost 4 million by 2010,[22] who not only required far greater military control and political pacification than did the Palestinian remnant living within Israel's pre-1967 borders[23] but also presented the Jewish state with a political conundrum to do with the future make-up of its people and the future character of its political regime. If Israel were to deny the inhabitants of the Occupied Territories citizenship in its body politic, it would have to rule those inhabitants as a permanent military despot instead of as the Western-style liberal democracy it prides itself on being. If Israel were to grant equal Israeli citizenship to those inhabitants, it could not maintain its self-rule as a Jewish state for very long, not to speak of having to buck the religious right's rejection of the principle of natural equality between Jews and non-Jews and the secular right's rejection of the principle of political fraternity between Jews and Arabs. If Israel were to retract the territory under its sovereign power to its pre-Occupation borders to preserve its ethno-religious constitution of "the people," it would lose land to which its right wing openly had laid claim and for which its left wing more discretely had longed from the beginning. Moreover, it would gain a next-door neighbor beyond its sovereign control, whose experience of the Israeli Occupation would have given it every reason to be hostile.[24]

The second continuity in foundational violence between 1948 and the post-1967 period is the massive destruction of Palestinian material existence within the expanding borders of the Israeli state. Jeff Halper, head of the Israeli Committee Against House Demolitions (ICAHD), notes this continuity when he reports that the erasure of between 417 and 536 Palestinian villages from 1948 into the 1960s has its analogue in the demolition of almost 23,000 Palestinian houses between 1967 and 2009,[25] not to speak of, after the start of the second Intifada in 2000, Palestinian roads, water pipelines, electrical grids, and hundreds of thousands of fruit and olive trees.[26] Almost all these demolitions, according to Halper and other Israeli critics, are both a form of collective punishment for Palestinian resistance to the Occupation and a method of compacting Palestinians into small, disconnected enclaves while clearing land around those enclaves for Jewish use.

To convey the assaultive process in more detail (although numbers can do only so much to convey the trauma), Halper offers the following statistics. In the wake of the 1967 war Israel evicted 300 Arab families from the Jewish Quarter of Jerusalem, destroyed two mosques and the homes of 135 Palestinian families in the Muslim quarter "to create a plaza for Jewish worshippers in front of the Western Wall," and razed at least 2,000 homes west of Jerusalem, covering them with a park. In 1971, to facilitate the movement of military vehicles, it crushed 2,000 houses in the Gaza refugee camps. It demolished 2,000 homes in the Occupied Territories in the late 1980s and early 1990s while quelling the first Intifada, 1,700 more during the Oslo Peace Process (1993–2000), and almost 5,000 during the second Intifada.[27] As one Israeli bulldozer driver described his part in demolishing 800 homes in the Jenin refugee camp in 2002: " 'For three days I just erased and erased.' "[28]

As a third continuity in foundational violence, the resettlement in 1948 of Jewish immigrants on former Palestinian property prefigures the rapid growth of Jewish settlements in the Occupied Territories, sometimes instigated by national-religious settlers and sometimes planned and promoted by the state. Before Israel dismantled Jewish settlements in Gaza in 2005, the number of Jewish settlers had reached 195,000, not including those moving into East Jerusalem, which Israel had annexed outright after the war along with the 64 surrounding square kilometers belonging to 28 Palestinian villages.[29] By the beginning of 2013, the number of Jewish settlers in the West Bank and East Jerusalem had climbed to 520,000.[30] As I write these lines, a new Jewish apartment complex is being proposed as "infill" in the Arab neighborhood of East Jerusalem, and plans have been announced to build 3,000 new Jewish houses in Greater East Jerusalem bisecting the West Bank.[31] Just as Israel, in the first year of its existence, had used the law to give Jews a right to the land of Arab "absentees," it has made use of legal mechanisms promulgated without the consent of Palestinians in the Occupied Territories to turn much of their land into Jewish property. According to Eyal Weizman, in addition to expropriating Palestinian land by military decree, by the early 1990s Israel had registered 38 percent of primarily the high ground of the West Bank as "state land" by resurrecting an old Ottoman Land Law of 1858, which stipulated that land not cultivated for three years automatically became property of the sovereign. Along with cultivated plots for which individual Palestinian owners could not prove title, the state then distributed this uncultivated land to Jewish hilltop settlements for their future expansion.[32]

A fourth continuity in foundational violence on both sides of the 1967 divide is the spatial separation of Jews and Arabs. Although Neve Gordon shows us that separation only emerged as Israel's control mechanism of choice in the Occupied Territories after the start of the second Intifada, separation is in fact no more than a materialization of the purported ontological distinction between Jews and Arabs that has been from the beginning the foundation of all foundational

violence in the Jewish state. The main mechanism of separation in
the pre-Occupation period was the classic contiguous nation-state
boundary line distinguishing Israel from the larger Arab region,
supplemented by more informal horizontal separations between intra-
national Jewish and Palestinian neighborhoods. In the post-2001
period, as Weizman shows us, a stricter separation occurs along three
different planes. Vertically, in much of the West Bank, Jewish deep
aquifer rights, Palestinian shallow water rights, Jewish-only transportation tunnels, and (illegal) Palestinian tunnels are layered on top of
one another below ground; Palestinian neighborhoods are admin-
istered by Palestinian officials in the flat valleys; Jewish settlements
perch on hilltops, subject to normal Israeli law; and Jewish-controlled
airspace sits atop everything else. Diagonally, Jewish-only roadways
and bridges span impoverished Palestinian neighborhoods in patterns
that hide Palestinian life from the sight of Jewish commuters as they
drive from Jewish enclaves in the West Bank to "mainland" Israel.
Horizontal barriers zigzag around these topographical labyrinths to
make up the ever-lengthening "separation wall," with its bump-out
loops sealing off as many Jewish settlements as possible, along with the
rest of the Jewish population, from concentrated Palestinian areas as
well as from (as in the case of a newly-envisioned wall on the Syrian
border) political upheavals in adjacent Arab countries. Finally, milita-
rized checkpoints, at which crowds of Palestinians wait for hours while
"Jewish settlers cruise unhindered through separate gates and down
protected corridors,"[33] inhibit and at times prohibit the movement of
Palestinians from the Occupied Territories to Israel or from one cut-off
section of the Territories to another. These segregated residential areas,
roadways, barriers, checkpoints, and, most recently, bus lines[34] have
an explicit security and an implicit ideological function. The security
function is to protect Israeli Jews from the non-violent as well as violent
protests of Palestinians—in other words, to protect the victors in the
struggle for sovereign power from the anger of the vanquished. The
ideological function is to cement the notions of victor and vanquished
as two alien and differently valued species of beings.

Each of the key continuities between the emergence of Israel in 1948 and its actions after 1967—the creation of a refugee population, the erasure of Palestinian material culture, the settlement of Jews in areas once inhabited by Arabs, and the separation of Jews and Arabs—distantly recalls foundational violence in North America. They also echo a lesson we learned from the American case, that the foundational violence entailed in the establishment of a sovereign nation-state is not confined to the state's original "birthday."

Settler colonialism was the method by which the Zionist movement acquired and expanded the boundaries of a Jewish sovereign state, fomenting in response the desire for freedom in a population displaced from its habitat and subjected to almost half a century of military occupation much crueler than this chapter was designed to convey. A state under permanent siege has been the outcome of that method and response. In turn, as David Lloyd and others have argued, the Israeli state has offered a new model of hyper-fortified sovereign politics for all liberal democratic states in the "age of terror."[35] All this is true, and yet the desire for liberation from oppression, not the desire either to oppress or to live under siege, was the original impetus to the Jewish search for sovereign power. To comprehend that desire, we must step outside the limits of a "settler colonial" analysis and begin the second part of our story.

The search for Jewish sovereign freedom

We shall live at last as free men on our own soil, and die peacefully in our own homes. The world will be freed by our liberty, enriched by our wealth, magnified by our greatness. And whatever we attempt to accomplish for our own welfare, will react powerfully and beneficially for the good of humanity—Theodor Herzl, *The Jewish State*

Anyone familiar with modern Jewish history should be struck by another curious resemblance besides the resemblance between foundational violence in America and Palestine. This is the resemblance between the relegation of Palestinians *by* Jews in the present and the relegation *of* Jews in the past to the position of despised Other. The dispersal of refugees into a world-wide diaspora; the use of state force and law to expropriate the property of one ethno-religious group for the benefit of another; the geographical transfer or articulated wish to transfer human beings as if they were objects; the confinement of a putatively alien-by-nature population to separate, walled off, impoverished quarters; the circulation of notions of ethno-racial superiority and purity, which periodically give rise, as if in a chemical reaction, to spontaneous physical assaults[36]—in short, the punishment of people for being who they are and where they are—all these practices have in Israel their distinctive origin, development, rationale, and proximate triggers. Nevertheless, they eerily evoke the treatment to which European Jews once were subjected before the quantitative increase in anti-Semitic offenses had taken that final, fatal qualitative leap. If such evocations are shocking when viewed from one angle, from another angle they are unsurprising. This is not simply because of the human inclination to make prejudicial we/they distinctions but also because the Jews learned the lesson of what it takes to be a free people from their former overlords.[37]

While the trials of the Jews are too complex to detail here, something can be said about the bookend episodes of the modern story that culminates in Zionism's birth. The first bookend is noteworthy for the date of its occurrence, its reference backwards to sheer religious hatred and forwards to the identitarian temptations of the sovereign nation-state, and its testimony to former mutual sympathies between peoples now at odds. In the same year that Christopher Columbus set sail for what would become "America," the last remnant of Moorish power in Granada was defeated by the Catholic Reconquista. That defeat was disastrous not only for Muslims but also for Jews, who had flourished for many years during Arab rule over the Iberian Peninsula. In what could be seen as the beginning of modern race politics, the sovereign monarchs Ferdinand and Isabella instigated an inquisition that found blood, not belief, the ultimate proof of religious faith, followed by their purification of Christian Spain by expelling alien elements from its territory. Of the Jews who made it out alive, many fled to the Arab Maghreb and the Ottoman imperial cities of Istanbul, Salonica, and Sarajevo, where they became a welcomed part of the tapestry of cosmopolitan, multi-ethnic urban life.[38]

The second bookend, more than three centuries later, was the so-called Jewish Emancipation, a series of halting steps by liberalizing European states to emancipate the Jews from their restricted ghetto life by bestowing equal civic and political rights on them. The invitation to political assimilation, however, opened the door to social suspicions of every trait Jews exhibited or alternatively were thought to be masking that was "racially" particularistic rather than in line with the national people's proclivities, sensibilities, and beliefs. Meanwhile, in the decades before and after Zionism emerged as a distinguishable tendency, romantic nationalist movements across Europe declared ties to the soil, folk culture, and ethno-religious identity the basis of political community[39]; pan-nationalist movements touting blood and belonging contested the legitimacy of multinational continental empires; and anti-colonial movements against overseas European imperialism drew on ethnic imagery to constitute their respective peoples. In this political atmosphere, it is hardly surprising that nationalism might come to seem the only effective remedy for an ethno-religious minority at the mercy of national majority prejudices regardless of legal equalizing measures.[40] Given the ongoing universalization of the modern nation-state form, the rise of nationalist movements even in the once hospitable-to-difference Ottoman Empire, the unique situation of the Jews as a minority in every actual and prospective nation-state, and the self-image of Jewish religious exclusivity, the conclusion of at least some Jews that the freedom of all Jews was contingent on their ascent to sovereign power inside a national territory of their own thus seems in retrospect almost foregone. Although a few "empty sites" in Argentina and Uganda were briefly considered, the choice of Palestine was also predictable in retrospect. Nationalist movements may emerge in reaction to real collective suffering, but they must galvanize their would-be peoples on the basis of a myth. A return from exile to Zion was the only mythic idea with the magnetism to galvanize traditional Eastern European Jews trapped in an impoverished and increasingly insecure ghetto life, Central and Western European Jews once their hopes had been dashed that their efforts at assimilation would bring them acceptance and love, and Oriental Jews who, while they had been belittled rather than crushed in Arab countries, were pitched into a more difficult situation once Israel was born.

If the idea of a "natural right of the Jewish people to be masters of their own fate, like all other nations, in their own sovereign State"[41] sparked the imagination of only a few individuals politicized by anti-Semitism in the early 1880s, it became alluring to many more over the next 50 years with each new wave of anti-Jewish state legislation and popular pogroms, especially once this "push" factor was fused with the promise of a return to the Holy Land as the "pull," the tireless efforts of organization and agitation on the part of Zionist activists being a crucial third factor. After the rise of Nazism and the refusal of other countries to save Jewish refugees from its horrors en masse, most of world Jewry was won over to the cause of winning sovereign power in Palestine at any cost.[42]

The passion for sovereign power for its own sake has a relatively straightforward psychological basis and dynamic. The thirst for wealth and honor and every other good that sovereign mastery promises to bring in its wake, the competitive drive to win supremacy over one's peers and turn them into one's inferiors, even the acceptance of inherited prerogative, which veils power urges in ornamental costume and weighs down those who wear jeweled crowns with obligations to their inferiors—all are variations of a desire to derive benefits for the self over against others that is no more mysterious than the opposite desire to enjoy the company of others without ruling, besting, or destroying them. While these twin desires are never unmediated by social conditions, they are elemental in the sense of flowing directly from the existential situation of the self as simultaneously separate from and drawn to other selves, and vulnerable to those other selves on both counts.

The passion for sovereign power as the solution to oppression, persecution, and humiliation, is, so to speak, a secondary reaction of the self to its vulnerability to the other and as such involves new psychological and social complications. Those complications are not difficult to decode when the enslaved self (if I might use the master/slave image metaphorically) desires sovereign power simply to turn the tables on his master, in order to enjoy all the pleasures of domination that were previously denied him.[43] Obviously, this desire can have unfortunate consequences for the master, especially as *ressentiment* foments a vindictive approach to rule, and it also can injure the slave by trapping him inside his revenge obsessions. Still, the slave who becomes the master of his former master achieves essentially what he has aimed at, and in that sense his victory produces no real surprises for us or for him.

The passion for sovereign power as the solution to oppression is more problematic, and the route towards its actualization is more tortuous, when the slave wishes not to invert but to transcend the master/slave relationship, to take his rightful place as a self-determining subject who governs himself according to his own lights, equally with every other free subject in the world. In this case, the enslaved self's worst fate is not imprisonment in an inverted master/slave relation that he longs for but imprisonment in a new master/slave relation that he fails to anticipate but is forced to initiate as soon as he acts to defeat forces hostile to his will. If beautiful ideals infuse the slave's original desire for sovereign freedom outside all master/slave dynamics, political inexperience and naïveté at once encourage those ideals and set up the slave for inevitable disenchantment. The slave's myopic focus on his own situation, which can blind his eyes to the impact of his actions on others and close his heart to felt concern for them, helps to tarnish the "beautiful" struggle for sovereign freedom, too.[44]

Of course, in real life desires are never cut and dried, and the human heart has its very dark chambers. Therefore it is not impossible, and perhaps not improbable, that the enslaved self wishes to transcend the master/slave relationship at the conscious level but at the unconscious level wishes to invert it.[45]

Before the state of Israel was anything more than a distant and vaguely articulated dream, no Zionist would have said, and few were likely to secretly think, that the Jews should gain sovereign freedom so that they could enjoy the pleasures of mastery by foisting the pains of subjugation onto someone else. The vice that most Zionists could most fairly be accused of was utter self-absorption, which fed a tendency to imagine a space for Jewish sovereign freedom in which no one else was there, or at least a space in which those who were there were magically reconciled to Jewish national aspirations. Because freedom for the Jews was the pivot around which the early Zionist imagination turned, an analysis of the oppression of the Jews that made their freedom urgent was the centerpiece of many classic Zionist texts. Regardless of one's view of the Zionist prescription for acquiring freedom, the Zionist diagnosis of the social illness that begged for an effective prescription of *some* sort should and, one hopes, would have been welcomed as an important contribution to the general critique of marginality, subordination, and degradation were it not for three countervailing factors. The first factor was the Zionists' fixation on the plight of the Jews, which disinclined them to extend their insights to the situation of other beleaguered minorities. The second factor was the Zionists' exaggeration of the difference between the Jews who had no homeland and all other minorities who could be said to have a country to return to if they were in desperate straits—but perhaps the exaggeration is more obvious *as* an exaggeration today, when economic destitution in so many "homelands" has pushed even majority peoples into social marginality, and when political cruelty keeps driving millions more into flight. However, the most potent factor preventing Zionist insights from being absorbed into the larger critical literature on the politics of domination and exclusion is the part Zionism has played in the practical recapitulation of those politics. The dismissal of Zionist voices on such grounds is unfortunate, as those voices not only illuminate the political psychology of oppression but also exemplify the logic that leads from oppression to the search for sovereign freedom to a new oppression.

The two major and one minor Zionists we shall highlight here to reveal that political psychology and logic—Theodore Herzl, Vladimir (Ze'ev) Jabotinsky, and Albert Memmi—have been selected in part because their writings offer complementary insights into the plight of the cultural minority, which in turn set the stage for a defense of sovereign power as the route to freedom for the Jews. Certain aspects of their early political formation are complementary, too. Each man was a secularist who once had been enamored of Western universalistic ideals, whether in the liberal idiom of freedom, the socialist idiom of equality and fraternity, or the cosmopolitan idiom of "world" (i.e. European) culture and citizenship. Each man suffered intense disillusionment when those lofty ideals turned out to be empty phrases at odds with brutal realities. As Memmi poignantly put it: "Encamped on the pink clouds of the Universal, for a long while I passionately asserted that man, in his heart, was one, that all men were brothers, generous and equal. Down on earth, however, a real and difficult battle was in progress, whose blows I was hardly able to avoid and hardly ever able to return."[46] Such a passage just as easily could have been Herzl's or Jabotinsky's, although neither directly received the vicious blows that Memmi did. There was also a reactive quality to each man's embrace of Jewish nationalism. One gets the strong impression of Zionism not only as a counter to inhumanity against the Jews in general but also as a personal repudiation of a repudiation, a method of assuaging the unrequited love of these three Jews for the particular societies that had rejected them. And yet all were able to light on Zionism because they had imbibed from those same societies the idea that the cure for the wounds inflicted on oppressed by dominant peoples lay in injecting the wounded with the virus of national exclusivity and power. Still, of the three men, only Jabotinsky was convinced that the wounded must acquire the capacity and willingness to wound, even if that meant having to become a full-time "Whipper." Otherwise, "if you want to be good, let yourself be killed: and renounce everything you would like to defend: home, country, freedom, hope."[47]

As Jabotinsky's sentiment signals, our thinkers also differ from one another in ways that are important, even if those differences prove that a wide variety of contextual situations and personal proclivities can issue in the same basic political conclusion. This variety is partly one of time and place. Herzl was born in 1860 to a German-acculturated middle class Jewish family in the Austro-Hungarian city of Budapest, studied law in Vienna, and as a journalist with the Viennese *Neue Freie Presse* was sent to Paris, where the anti-Semitic private slurs, public speeches, and career restrictions that until then had simmered at the lower levels of his consciousness were finally brought to a boil. Jabotinsky was born 20 years after Herzl, further east, in Odessa, where he fell in love with Russian literature; he studied law in Rome, where he fell in love with Italian nationalism; and, while embarking on a promising literary career as a foreign newspaper correspondent, poet, editor, linguist, and translator, was inducted into Zionist politics through his involvement with Russian Zionists who were organizing in response to the 1903 Kishinev pogrom. Memmi, the outlier of the three, was born 40 years after Jabotinsky on the edge of a poor Jewish ghetto in Tunisia. Although active as a boy in Zionist youth groups, he was immersed in the culture of the Maghreb, identifying during the colonial period with Arabs against the West and with poor Jews and Arabs against the wealthy classes, including Frenchified Jews. Imprisoned as a Jew in a forced labor camp in Vichy-ruled Tunisia and then meeting anti-Jewish and anti-Arab prejudice while studying philosophy in Paris after the war, Memmi returned to Tunisia to join the nationalist movement. He departed again for France when he saw no place for Jews in a free Tunisia that centered the first article of its Constitution on its identity as a Muslim state.[48]

The relationship of each man to the Zionism movement is also distinct. Herzl not unjustifiably saw Jewish nationalism as his brainchild[49] and was obsessed with the material conditions of its realization from the mid-1890s until his early death in 1904. He published his mobilizing tract, *The Jewish State* (*Der Judenstaat*) in 1896,[50] organized and presided over the first World Zionist Congress in 1897, and crusaded tirelessly thereafter for a Jewish Homeland among Jewish philanthropists (who showed little interest), world leaders (who gave a few promises but very little real support), and poor Jewish masses, who were his most receptive audience.[51] Jabotinsky believed himself Herzl's truest heir. He was a charismatic, peripatetic, and highly controversial figure who championed the Zionist cause in a dazzling number of languages and through a prolific output of speeches, articles, and organizing efforts in Russia, Europe, North and South Africa, Turkey, and North America, as well as in Palestine until the British banned him from there in 1930 because of his incendiary politics. He helped found and lead the right-wing World Union of Zionist Revisionists, for which the nation was not merely the supreme but the sole principle; acted as head and mentor for a Jewish military youth organization, *Betar*; and agitated for armed Jewish self-defense and ultimately armed struggle against whomever he saw as an enemy of the Jews, as well as for the territorial expansion of Jewish colonization in Palestine and unrestricted, i.e. illegal, Jewish immigration.[52] Unlike Herzl and Jabotinsky, Memmi was a follower of Zionism rather than a leader, and moreover a follower from afar. He was an Oriental as opposed to a European Jew, and a Jew who chose to remain in the despised (by the Zionists) diaspora. Memmi's searing portraits in *The Colonized and the Colonizer* of the mentalities produced by colonialism—for the painting of which "all I needed to do ... was to call up my own memories and contemplate the scars"[53]—gained him fame among anti-colonial nationalists across the globe. He is less touted for using the same provocative pen in *The Portrait of the Jew, The Liberation of the Jew,* and *Jews and Arabs* as well as in his autobiographical novels to convey the problems of Jewish minorities in North Africa and France.[54] Memmi came to defend the Jewish state as a necessary if not sufficient condition of the dissolution of those problems, declaring Israel essential to the liberation of an oppressed people and "part of the destiny of every Jew anywhere in the world who continues to acknowledge himself as a Jew."[55]

Aside from but informing how each understood his Zionist commitments, the three men ran a long ideological gamut. Herzl was an aristocratic, optimistic, modernity-infatuated liberal. While disdainful of the shallow and self-interested rich (as he complained in his diaries, "All the prosperous Jews are against me"[56]), he was equally appalled by the prospect of a workers' revolution and was not above raising the specter of an incendiary Jewish working-class to convince others to back Zionism as the more moderate option. Jabotinsky, who admired capitalists and was even more hostile to socialist revolutionaries than Herzl had been, had the intellectual temperament of an austere Nietzschean,[57] valorizing the noble virtues of physical strength, mental fortitude, pride, courage, chivalry, and self-discipline, and vacillating between heroic individualism ("In the beginning, God created the individual, a king who is equal among kings,"[58] and no state should interfere with the "royalty" of every man over his "individual 'kingdom' "[59]) and proto-fascism ("There is nothing in the world more valuable than Iron,"[60] an "unjust strike ... harmful to the State, must be mercilessly squashed,"[61] and "a mass of free people ... can function with the absolute, utter precision of a machine"[62]). Memmi, in contrast, was influenced by Marxism, although he concluded from his experience of European colonialism that the psychic life of racism was no less central to modern politics than economic exploitation. He stood far from Herzl and even farther from Jabotinsky in taking up the cause of not just Jews or national minorities but all species of "dominated men."[63]

Perhaps as a reflection of their clashing ideologies, these three figures exhibit different attitudes with respect to the sovereign freedom/domination nexus. Herzl was almost completely blind to that nexus, seeming to believe not only that the slave can become a master without negative effects on anyone else but also that everyone living in the vicinity of the new master would rally as supporters of his efforts and reap much-appreciated benefits from them. In his utopian novel, *Altneuland* (in which even a German nobleman sings the praises of an imaginary Jewish state), Herzl went so far as to have a fictional Arab declare: " 'Jewish immigration was a blessing for all of us.' "[64] Jabotinsky, being much more steely-eyed, understood that a Jewish state very definitely would not be considered a blessing by the Arabs and did not hesitate to call for sovereign domination of the resistant Other as the path to freedom for the self.[65] Between those positive and negative poles, Memmi was alert to the dark side of sovereign freedom and considered those in harm's way with a sensitivity that Jabotinsky never had the inclination to muster. He admitted that nationalism "is far too frequently an alibi for hatred and domination," wrung his hands over its inevitable "contraction of a people within themselves," lamented the Jews' "collectively neurotic choice" of a site for their state in an "already inhabited, terribly exposed corner of earth."[66] Still, he endorsed Jewish sovereign power over that corner, if only as a "temporary ending" during a historical stage in which peoples fortified themselves against one another in separate nation-states,[67] to be one day surpassed, he hoped, by a "binational or even anational symbiosis."[68]

From sovereign freedom to sovereign domination

Young men, learn to shoot!—Vladimir Jabotinsky

"In the beginning is the idea," Herzl announced in his opening address at the Fifth Zionist Congress, and the very existence of that Congress, whose members came annually from many parts of the world to help turn the idea of a Jewish state into actuality, seemed to testify to the truth of that claim.[69] Yet in hindsight, one also might have suspected that Herzl's faith in the primacy of ideas over material reality was what caused him to overlook the conflicts that Jewish sovereignty in Palestine was likely spark, were it not for the equally strong belief in the power of ideas of Jabotinsky,[70] who could foresee exactly what the real-life trouble was going to be. And, of course, one need only recall that famous non-Zionist revolutionary leader who also was convinced that an idea could change or at least speed up the course of history once it had found its dedicated human vessel, whether that vessel was a collective mass, a vanguard party, or a single determined man. What distinguished Vladimir Lenin from Herzl, both of whom held to the same idea/human vessel formula, was Lenin's combative world-view, his first-hand familiarity with the social and political terrain on which his ideal was to be made real, and his solid grasp of the forces that would be arrayed against the effort. It was not, then, Herzl's faith that an idea wildly at odds with empirical reality could become empirical reality that explains his erroneous supposition that the whole world would embrace the Jewish state. It was rather his liberal progressive outlook, which led him to marry an energizing "optimism of the will" to a dangerously misleading "optimism of the intellect"; his physical and cultural distance from the actual geographical site for his plans; and, finally, his assumption that imperial powers were the only forces that really mattered in world affairs, and their leaders the only ones it was crucial to win over.

But if Herzl was naïve about the realities that would have to be overcome to actualize his idea in that portion of the Ottoman Empire on which Zionism had trained its eye, he was far from naïve about realities in Europe that prompted that idea in the first place. He knew that European societies were unwilling to embrace their Jewish populations whether or not they had given them equal civic and political rights, and that they had or would soon have a strong interest in shipping most of their Jews elsewhere. Admittedly, even on this last point Jabotinsky would prove more of a realist than Herzl, when he wrote in 1940 (and to be sure, things in Europe had gotten much worse by then) that sadism simultaneously hates and "does not wish to lose its victim." It was one of the "mysteries of mass-psychology," Jabotinsky noted, that racial hatred of the Jews made their presence at least for a while more desirable to society than their absence. That hatred could be likened to "a spice or sauce which enables the masses to swallow a species of poison which would be too corrosive without it ... the piquant sauce which accelerates both the swallowing and the digestion of ideas and policies" that otherwise would be unpalatable to those forced to consume them.[71]

In the beginning is, then, not the idea but the background reality that provokes the idea and makes its actualization seem imperative. The background reality that first badly jolted Herzl, or at least epitomized for him the reason why his Jewish readers should be badly jolted, were popular demonstrations in 1897 against bringing the French Jewish officer Alfred Dreyfus back from Devil's Island so that he could defend himself against trumped-up charges of treason.[72] "The people of France, the magnanimous people which is in love with justice, the people of the rights of man ... [did] not wish to have the guilt of the Jewish captain even called into question ... They did not howl 'Down with Dreyfus!' but 'Down with the Jews!' "[73]

The rage with which the French people condemned a minority group for the suspected sins of an individual, who was suspect precisely because he was a member of that group, did not prompt Herzl to rethink the value of popular sovereignty in the political sense of the term, for he had dismissed Rousseauist ideals of popular social contract and democratic law-making in the first place, declaring that societies owed both their foundations and their day-to-day rule to a small number of leaders, "directors," or "gestors."[74] But Herzl did rethink the principles of universal freedom, fraternity, and equal treatment in which he *had* believed, on the grounds that, in every existing political order in the civilized world, it was an ethnic (or ethno-religious or racial) majority people that turned out to be sovereign in the social sense. Unlike Arendt in her own response to the Dreyfus case half a century later, Herzl was never tempted to salvage the popular ideal by distinguishing "the People" from "the Mob," the first faithful to an inclusive, republican notion of nationhood and the second lashing out against the secret machinations of racially alien insiders. He suggested instead that every national people could be induced to support, incite, or metastasize into a mob against an identifiable minority living in its midst. When the chips were down, the difference between (French) civic and (German) ethnic constitutions of "the people" proved to be merely apparent.

To the political fact Herzl had discovered that "the people" is inevitably an ethnically particular category, Jabotinsky appended the "human nature" fact that every self preferred its own ethnic group to the rest of humanity. *His* qualm about popular sovereignty, while rooted in his penchant for strong leaders, also stemmed from his awareness that nothing in the most democratic constitution of a sovereign people prevented it from oppressing those not considered part of the sovereign popular body. But if Herzl and Jabotinsky gleaned their understanding of normality from the ethnic exclusivity they saw in the world around them, their belief that the ideal had to remain within the limits of normality goes a long way to explaining why they thought that no political organization could liberate the Jews except one based on the principle of ethnonational particularity.

Three aspects stand out in Herzl's analysis of actually existing anti-Semitism, each acquiring a Jabotinskian supplement. Each aspect also, incidentally, finds a later echo in Arendt's own writings on the subject. Indeed, Arendt congratulates Herzl for recognizing anti-Semitism as a political problem requiring some kind of political solution, even as she slams him for swallowing German nationalist presumptions about peoples "as biological organisms mysteriously endowed with eternal life," for touting "an unchanging hostility toward the Jews that was ready to take the form of pogroms or persecution at any moment," and for conspiring with imperialist powers to achieve his aims.[75]

Modern anti-Semitism, according to Herzl, while grafted onto traditional religious intolerance, was not a function of the religious antipathy that Christians felt towards Jews. Instead, it arose in response to a more amorphous Jewish "difference" that became a popular irritant once states decided to undo "the inhumanity of discriminatory legis-lation" against the Jews.[76] The emancipation proclamations of those states proved not merely "friendlier than customs."[77] They exacerbated the customary hostility of native majorities as soon as cultural strangers freed to make their way as equal individuals of society became more accomplished than the native professional middle classes, or richer than the native economic elites, or poorer and more dangerously revolutionary than the native proletariat, or, in their creative endeavors, matchlessly clever at imitating a national cultural "original."[78] Just a few decades of deteriorating circumstances gave Jabotinsky greater cause to dismiss the effectiveness of legal equalities in the face of anti-Semitism, as the equal rights of minorities enshrined in law between 1871 and 1919 in the German Empire, Austro-Hungary, Poland, Czechoslovakia, and the Baltic states did nothing to halt and arguably something to spur that racial hatred. Jabotinsky also added crisp details to Herzl's generalities about the economic jealousy that arose among Gentiles once Jews were allowed to compete freely with them. Equal rights mean "the right to win if you are better equipped," wrote this enthusiast of all competitive battles,[79] who once declared (albeit with some thought about ameliorating the process): "Humanity must always be stormy and seething … one will rise to the heights, another will slide down the precipice."[80] However, no equal legal right could protect, for example, "better equipped" urban Jews from the resentment of Polish peasants flocking to the cities in search of work in a period of increasing industrial unemployment.[81] What we today would term the structural determinants of the persecution of minorities, Jabotinsky dubbed the "anti-Semitism of things" (in distinction from subjective feelings of repulsion or the "anti-Semitism of men"): objective conditions that encourage the ostracism of the Jew "almost independent of whether his neighbors like or dislike him."[82]

In turn, Herzl insisted on the impossibility of Jewish assimilation into Gentile society. Assimilation was a dead end for Jews in large part because of the Christian majority's rejection of them, for true assimilation is, in Jabotinsky's words, a "duet," not a "solo performance."[83] But equally prohibitive was the demand that the individual who wished to re-train himself for either a duet *or* a solo part in this new orchestra cut his ties to his old community or at least turn his Judaism into a purely private affair. The paradox as Herzl saw it was that ghetto Jews were bound to one another by both shared traditions and a shared plight in which they were "without honour, without rights, without justice, without defense," while Jews who enjoyed "freedom, liberty and equality presented to them as a gift by the civilized world … ceased to be Jews." The sacrifice of the "warmth of community" for individual freedom was worse than an exchange of a loss for a gain, for that exchange meant that the individual would be stranded on his own when the larger society turned its back on him. This is why, Herzl concluded, "a man, to be a man, must have both freedom and the feeling of community."[84]

Finally, Herzl characterized the Jews as a "surplus" population, initially in the most anti-Semitic countries, then in neighboring states to which they fled when conditions at home had become too oppressive, and finally in societies they tried to reach after hearing that other Jews lived freely and happily there. Ultimately, he warned, even liberal England and the United States would become, as the result of massive immigration, as inhospitable as Germany, Austria, Poland, and Russia. "[T]ossed from country to country"[85] with "their miserable bundles,"[86] the Jews were fated to bring the "bundle" of anti-Semitism along with them, eliciting at their point of arrival the antipathies that they were trying to escape at their point of departure. Every place, Herzl noted, "can tolerate a certain number of Jews ... once this indeterminate number is exceeded, anti-Semitism cries out: Stop!"[87] Or, to paraphrase Jabotinsky's blunter words, "No one wants the Jewish tramp."[88]

To these sociological factors—the incompatibility of political equality and social difference, a doomed assimilation process, and the multiplier effect of being branded as a surplus population by any one nation-state—Jabotinsky adds what he sees as three unpleasant truths about human psychology. The ugliest truth is that some people are sadists who enjoy seeing a hated race "squirming and writhing beneath one's feet." The most historically specific truth is that, once the ideas of humanity and equality have been embedded in culture, a "formidable effort" is required to make a "clean sweep" of those ideas so that leaders can "send the masses to their death, and to massacre others." Modern racial ideologies are the fruit of that effort. But the most "elemental and primordial" truth is the special sympathy everyone feels for "one's own people" and everyone's consequent willingness to sacrifice the alien in times of distress, on the calculation that "'it's either my son or the Jew's son, for there's only one loaf.'"[89] Jabotinsky attaches to this self-preferring instinct a disclaimer he repeats whenever he tries to force the hard facts of life on the politically inexperienced Jews (about whose leaders Herzl once had written: "Report card: Arithmetic: Excellent; Politics: Poor"[90]). The preference for kin over strangers, according to Jabotinsky, "is definitely not praiseworthy. It is disgraceful, bestial. Were I the ruler of the universe, instead of the Almighty, I would create an entirely different universe. I would never permit such a character-istic to develop. But it nevertheless exists, among Jews as well, and cannot be eradicated."[91]

Memmi lives late enough into the twentieth century and far enough outside the West to complicate Herzl and Jabotinsky's analysis of anti-Semitism by dissecting the "middling" instead of entirely abject position of the Jews in regions colonized by European countries. He describes the ghetto Jews of his native Tunis as "steering a course for a century between Arabs and Frenchmen, carefully locking their doors at night, but punctually celebrating their Sabbath ... poor, without recognized rights, but in spite of several alarms, almost at home." Sandwiched between colonizer and colonized, Tunisian Jews looked up to the French, but they led the same materially degraded lives that Muslim Arabs did, as well as sharing almost all of their habits, customs, sensibilities, and tastes. Regarded by the French with colonial contempt before Tunisian national independence, the Jews became a "civic and national negativity" afterwards. "The independence of Tunisia and of Morocco ... was not directed against the Jews, but neither was it made with the Jews ... It is in the very way in which new nations were born that differences became clear, were confirmed, showed us plainly that we were not part of it."[92] Anti-colonial nationalism, in short, unearthed a new version of the Jewish Question at the same moment that it buried the Colonial Question by forging "the people" in culturally singular terms.

According to Herzl—and while Memmi might have balked at the final clause of the definition, Jabotinsky would have not—a nation is "a historical group of people who recognizably belong together and are held together or driven together by a common foe."[93] It can be inferred from this proto-Schmittean proposition that a nation is oppressed when it is ruled by that same foe. When a national minority is oppressed by a majority, three pathways to freedom are theoretically open to it. The individual members of the nation can try to merge with their foe, but Herzl was adamant that this assimilation option was closed off to most Jews. The minority as a whole can rise up against its oppressors, but Herzl was hardly the type to endorse revolutionary action and in any event would have judged the chances of success for a minority revolt against a majority people to be suicidally slim.[94] The third pathway to freedom is the surgical excision of the minority from the oppressive society so that it might attain the status of a majority someplace else. This was the pathway Herzl set out on in 1896, Jabotinsky urged all Central and Eastern European Jews to take in 1940, and Memmi echoed in 1962 with reference to Jews in Arab countries, when he concluded that, if other peoples "are as yet unable to put up with the presence of compact minorities among them ... the Jew must be removed from their midst."[95]

There was something, however, about particularly Herzl's and Jabotinsky's prescriptions that smacked of a certain complicity between Zionism and anti-Semitism, and the suspicion that they trucked with anti-Semites was an unpleasantness that dogged them both. The medical language they used in describing Jews as a "painful abscess in the organisms of other nations,"[96] Zionism as "a kind of new Jewish care" for the "poor, sick Jewish people,"[97] and mass evacuation as "the only remedy for the cancer of Jewish distress"[98] was ambiguous about just who was making whom unhealthy, and why, if the Jews were suffering from the disease of anti-Semitism, they were the ones who had to be cut out like a tumor from the body of their host. In practice, Herzl counted on anti-Semitic animosity to induce the requisite number of Jews to desire their own state and indeed, given that "the enemy is the iron ring that holds a nation together,"[99] to see themselves as a nation in the first place. The anti-Semites, in sum, had to go on being anti-Semites to "create a desire to emigrate where it did not previously exist, and strengthen it where it existed before."[100] And, as Zionists would render "a patriotic service" in the "countries where the Jews are disliked,"[101] they could request and expect the help of "honest Anti-Semites" to ease the process of Jewish departure.[102]

If the details of this seamy underside of Zionism lie beyond the scope of this study, so do the details of the paradise that Herzl believed the Jews would erect. Suffice it to say that he anticipated a tolerant, humanistic, polyglot, worker-and-industrialist-friendly Jewish state based on the most advanced arts and sciences—a model of progress and justice for the rest of the world that Jabotinsky also envisioned, although with less emphasis on humanism and greater emphasis on Jewish particularity, emblemized in his demand that Hebrew be the sole national language of the Jewish people.

More pertinent for us are two other, final points. First, the Zionists were no more able than anyone else to evade the paradox of all political foundings, whether they occur through colonial settlement or not. Herzl registered this paradox both when he declared in *The Jewish State* that a "state is created by a nation's struggle for existence. In any such struggle it is impossible to obtain proper authority ... beforehand."[103] While he admitted in his diary that, like all other founders of states, "I conduct the affairs of the Jews without their mandate,"[104] the higher-rightlessness of all sovereign national right was exacerbated in the case of a diasporic people, whose members were too spread out over the globe to give a new state even the veneer of being grounded in the consensual agreement of its prospective citizens for which Arendt had praised the Americans. Thus Herzl believed that a small, self-selected Society of Jews would have to found the Jewish state in the name of the larger mass.[105]

Second, and specifically licensing colonial settlement, the members of a perpetual minority could "live at last as free men on our own soil, and die peacefully in our own homes" only if they were granted sovereignty "over a portion of the globe large enough to satisfy the rightful requirements of a nation." The consequence of such a grant seemed so unproblematic to Herzl that he predicted that the Jews not only would be free once they had their own territorial state but "would probably have no more enemies," or at least no more than "every nation has."[106]

Jabotinsky, being hyper-aware of the enemies that Jewish sovereign freedom was likely to incur precisely because of the territorial issue, comes much closer to embracing, for that reason, sovereign freedom and domination as an inseparable pair. I say "much closer," because although Jabotinsky acknowledges the dependence of sovereign freedom on the domination that procures and protects it, he denies that such domination is necessarily either unjust or unpleasant for the Other. The clash between that acknowledgment and that denial lends his commentary on relations between Zionist Jews and Palestinian Arabs a highly agitated quality.

Thus, on the one hand, Jabotinsky insists that the Jews must colonize Palestine on both sides of the Jordan River to accommodate the millions of immigrants who will require resettlement once the diaspora is entirely liquidated. He admits that, historically, colonization always has been accomplished without the consent of the colonized, and that "against colonization by an outside race, the local population always fights, everywhere and without exception."[107] Therefore the Jews will have to impose their "indomitable will-power" on Arabs by means of arms.[108] As Jabotinsky said with respect to the Zionists' conflict with the British colonial administration in Palestine but could equally have said about their conflict with the Arabs: "I abhor broken windows just like everyone else, broken heads even more … If it were in my power to create today's world, I would do it completely differently. However … [t]he world is what it is."[109] In any event, if colonial compulsion counts as a crime, "it follows that America is a crime, this country [England] is a crime, all Europe is a crime, and our Bible history is the story of a crime."[110]

As the Arab inhabitants of Palestine will naturally begrudge the loss of any of their native land to the Jews, between even the Zionist minimalists and the most moderate Arabs "there is no connecting bridge."[111] Therefore Zionists must create an "Iron Wall" with "no single loophole"[112] to force an agreement on the Arabs on the Jewish terms that, as Jabotinsky had articulated them as early as 1919, "everything glorious the land has to offer belongs to us—the Jewish nation."[113] The same

Iron Wall must protect Jewish national dominance in Eretz-Israel once this agreement has been reached, for "'[e]very distinctive race aspires to become a nation, to create a separate society, in which everything must be in this race's image—everything must accommodate the tastes, habits, and unique attributes of this specific race.'"[114] To express its individual spirit, every national people must own its own "'laboratory,' a land where the nation ... manages its own affairs and is free to adapt its communal life to its own ideas of what is good or not good."[115]

On the other hand, Jabotinsky claims that it is a righteous act for the Jewish "vagabond" to take a portion of "excess land" from the Arab nation, given that the Arabs possess vast and empty land holdings.[116] Furthermore, this vagabond can build its state without dislodging anyone else. Indeed, there is room for one million Arabs, another million of their offspring, and many more millions of Jewish immigrants to live within the same territorial boundaries, so that the Arabs should not feel the need to emigrate (although it wouldn't be "a tragedy or a disaster" if they did). Even if "it is pleasanter to be in the majority than the minority," a national minority "can live in reasonable contentment." As proof of Zionism's having "nothing to do with the will to dominate over anyone," the Jewish state should accord Arabs equal civil rights; a proportional share of Parliamentary seats, cabinet offices, court judgeships, and state benefits; equal legal status with Hebrew for the Arabic language; cultural autonomy with respect to religion, social assistance, and education; and equal access to holy sites and wasteland allotments.[117] However, the Jews must retain their standing as the sovereign national majority, the Arabs must live in the country as a permanent minority, and "Zion is all ours!"[118]

Historically, as we have seen, Jabotinsky's demand for Jewish sovereign freedom derives its positive charge from nineteenth-century ideals of ethnonational distinctiveness and self-determination, and its negative charge from the persecution of Jewish minorities by anti-Semitic states and national majorities. But philosophically, that demand has its roots in Jabotinsky's interconnected convictions that "men are almost gods," that "every man is a king," and that "I am a

King and claim my Kingly birthright."[119] The first conviction, that men are almost gods, elevates the human race nearly to the level of metaphysical sovereigns or, to put the point differently, secularizes theological sovereign power. The second conviction, that every man has a right to lordship on the grounds of his equality with all other men, implicates each man in an unresolvable contradiction, for no man can be a king unless other men are subjected to his will, whether by being subjugated inside the space over which that man is king or by being forbidden by that man to enter that space. The third conviction, that "I" am a king, attributes to Jabotinsky as a Jew this contradictory secular right. All the conundrums generated by the idea of sovereign power once it is brought down from the heavens and combined with the incompatible principle of human equality surface in Jabotinsky's call for Jewish sovereign freedom in Palestine. The same conundrums are compacted in a line Jabotinsky wrote just before his death. As if he were asserting, simultaneously, a right to equal treatment with every other human being on earth and an intention to exert sovereign mastery over all the earth, he proclaimed: "I insist on law and justice for myself; and if I do not receive it I shall overturn the world making it a desert and wasteland."[120]

A requiem for national self-determination

If the project of disentangling the members of an oppressed group from Europe so that they might live as they wished in Palestine was doomed to failure, this is not because of an eternal anti-Semitism that supposedly follows the Jews everywhere. The project was doomed because of the inevitability that a minority seeking sovereign status in a new geographical space would become entangled with inhabitants of that space who were bound to resent and reject that status. In truth, any subject seeking sovereign freedom—that is, the freedom to act according to its own will without being subjected to the pressure of the wills of other subjects—either will have to fly to a distant star or devote itself to crushing the capacity for free action of others here on earth, thereby becoming vulnerable to their warranted hostility. It thus is unsurprising that, to the same degree that Zionism succeeded in achieving Jewish sovereign power in Palestine, which as Jabotinsky was forthright enough to admit hinged on Jewish domination *over* Palestine, the Jews would meet the antagonism of Palestinian Arabs, which would have boomerang effects on the sovereign power and freedom of Israeli Jews, as the separation walls, military checkpoints, security barriers, segregated roadways and bus lines, and the surveillance labyrinth with which Israel has blanketed itself now testify. This time, however, the antagonism facing the Jews is a function of, not the hatred of the oppressor for the oppressed, which Jabotinsky once rightly pronounced poisonous and, at its outer edges, sadistic, but the anger of the oppressed at the oppressor, which the whole world understands and with which many in the world just as rightly feel sympathy.

Sometimes history is so unkind as to trumpet a compelling answer to a grave social problem that proves to be the wrong answer or at least an answer that creates new problems just as grave. Not only could it not supply its people with freedom in the sovereign sense of the term; the Jewish state did not succeed in bringing freedom in the different, Arendtian sense of the capacity to escape all objectively determined processes to create something new. Out of dedication, energy, and imaginative flair, the Zionists created a political society from scratch to establish what they saw as the precondition of freedom for an oppressed people. However, in grasping for themselves the prerogatives of national self-determination, they set in motion a relentless "bad dialectic" of aggressing and avenging forces, with, thus far, asymmetrically punishing outcomes but equally severe effects of self/ other alienation on both sides. There seems to be no light at the end of *this* tunnel. Would the triumph of the Palestinian struggle for sovereign freedom count as such a light? Certainly every lover of justice should wish the very best outcome for the Palestinian cause, even though the material conditions for an optimal outcome are shrinking every day. Still, not all the wishes in the world can inoculate a people on the sovereign power route to freedom from its own susceptibility to the warning we lifted earlier from Marx: "this story"—or some version of this story—"will be told about you!"

Epigraphs

Karl Marx, *Capital*, vol. 1, ed. Frederick Engels, trans. Samuel Moore and Edward Aveling (New York: International Publishers, 1967 [1867]), 8.

Franz Kafka, *The Trial*, trans. Willa Muir and Edwin Muir (New York: Modern Library, 1956 [1925]), 104–5.

Theodor Herzl, *The Jewish State: An Attempt at a Modern Solution of the Jewish Question* (New York: American Zionist Emergency Council, 1946 [1896]), 157.

Vladimir Jabotinsky, "Affen Pripatchook," *The Jewish Herald*, posthumous publication, September 12, 1947, excerpted in *The Political and Social Philosophy of Zeʾev Jabotinsky: Selected Writings*, ed. Mordechai Sarig, trans. Shimshon Feder (London: Vallentine Mitchell, 1999), 35.

Conclusions and Extrapolations

Intimations of non-sovereign freedom

Given that the conquest and rule of peripheral regions by imperial centers has typified much of the world for much of human history, it would be odd to claim that the West created empire as a political form. The more modest and accurate charge is that modern imperialism was born when Western nation-states began to look to overseas and continental European territories as their own exploitable possessions. Ironically, the West also provided the world with the sovereign nation-state model as the political answer to imperial penetration abroad as well as to the oppression of ethnic minorities at home. By centralizing political power over a territory with sacrosanct boundaries, a formerly subjugated or diminished people could hope to win negative freedom from outside interference and positive freedom in the sense of national and at least ostensibly popular self-rule.

The sovereign nation-state, however, has turned out to be no less problematic than its imperial predecessors. Although they benefited from asymmetrical relations between different peoples, empires by the same token were willing to accommodate heterogeneous collective identities with their own customs, beliefs, norms, and even self-referring laws. In contrast, the modern nation-state, while underwriting the solidarity and political-legal equality of its citizens, either championed the interests of a pre-existing homogeneous population at the expense of ethnic strangers or tried to weld together—via overtly or covertly coercive processes of assimilation, exclusion, or extermination—a homogeneous population out of the diverse elements it found in the territory it claimed for itself. Today, as multiplying pressures on its aspirations to impermeability and homogeneity make the sovereign nation-state seem more and more of a relic from another age, a new question demands its as-of-yet unfathomable answer. How might political communities be re-constituted to combine ethno-cultural heterogeneity, the "positive moment" of empire, with individual equality of legal protection and political voice, the "positive promise" of the nation-state?

Unfortunately, political psychological sensibilities that have hardened as a result of modern imperialism and modern nationalism present tremendous obstacles to such a synthesis. The Israeli/Palestinian conflict is a perfect case in point. The regional inequalities characteristic of the age of Western imperialism, the domestic furies unleashed by the homogeneity fetishism of the nation-state, and the passion for sovereign power as the antidote to both coalesced in the Jewish struggle for sovereign freedom and the Palestinian counter-struggle for the same putative good. The scars, as Memmi would put it, that their distinctive but interconnected experiences have left on Israeli Jews and Palestinian Arabs make it difficult to see how either party ever would be willing to participate in a joint project of any sort, not to speak of the project of creating a new entity in which each people could enjoy the practices to which it is attached, foster bonds of solidarity with one another, and exercise equal political agency. It would require an optimism of the intellect—one almost as great as Herzl's sunny estimate of how a new Jewish state would be greeted by its neighbors—to rely on the fact that history has taken unpredictable turns before, even when it had seemed fated to repeat a deterministic logic ad infinitum. The chances of a "miracle of action" with respect to any deep and recalcitrant conflict are by definition very slim. Still, it is possible to find rays of hope in actually existing exceptions to sovereign politics in Israel/Palestine that intimate what freedom could look like under conditions of *non*-sovereignty. Let me point very briefly to just two of those exceptions, in which those who have managed to wrest themselves free from rigid self/other antinomies attempt to engage in a relationship without exerting sovereign power against one another.

The first exception takes us back to the Israeli Committee Against House Demolitions, which we met in Chapter 3. Under the aegis of

that organization, Israeli Jews, Palestinians, and international volun-
teers have worked together to reconstruct (at least for the moment)
Palestinian domestic spaces bulldozed on orders of the Israeli
government. By their actions, these rebels reassert the Palestinians'
right to a physical home in the world that is one of freedom's bedrock
conditions. By those same actions, they also instantiate a miniature
multi-ethnic public more generous and worldly than one confined
to the members of a tight "family circle." Moreover, they do so not
by committing foundational violence but by restoring that which
was erased by foundational violence.[1] Through its efforts to exert
creative political agency against the destructive powers of the sovereign
ethnonational state, ICAHD can be said to be building a house where
freedom *actually* can live.

   Another intimation of non-sovereign freedom lies in the actions of
Palestinians in villages such as Bil'in,[2] who, flanked by Israeli leftists
and international peace activists, have protested weekly for years
against the West Bank barrier that separates them from their olive
groves and also against the ideological separation of human beings
into airtight and unequal categories. In confronting Israeli soldiers
and West Bank Jewish settlers with an insistence on their own right to
dignity, political agency, and economic sustenance, the villagers exert
the moral force of a self-organized popular body against sovereign
military force. Just as significantly, they demonstrate their recognition
of the Other's humanity by calling on the Other to respond to them
in a human way, even as that other is armed to the hilt and seems
impervious to their suffering. Anyone who has witnessed these weekly
confrontations should be forgiven for concluding that the enlargement
of freedom in this corner of the world hangs not on the success of
the Palestinian fight for sovereign power, but on the acceptance by
the Other of the villagers' invitation to step outside the limitations of
a sovereign/subject relationship and into a human-to-human frame.
To be sure, a human response to a human need by a single group of
soldiers would interrupt the downward spiral of a bad dialectic only
for a moment and only on a micro-level. But generalized throughout

society, such a miracle would have the best chance of paving the way to the emancipation of Palestinians from their restricted circumstances and the emancipation of Israeli Jews from the straitjacket that the struggle for sovereign freedom has designed for them.

Erasing the past

The destruction of familiar landscapes and the sentiments and social practices they support is not only a function of the founding of a new sovereign polity or the victory of one ethno-nationality over another. The bountiful winter hunting grounds and spring fishing waters of seventeenth-century Native Americans, and their ability to move freely from one to the other without being halted by fences, were as vulnerable to the development of a capitalist economy based on private property accumulation as they were to the territorial ambitions of the young United States. The olive groves so carefully tended by twenty-first-century Palestinian villagers are likely to be as jeopardized by an independent Palestinian state, if one is finally born and follows the typical pattern of modernization, as they have been by Israel's ethnonational expansion.

This raises, among other quandaries, the question of whether what Michael Oakeshott has called the love of the familiar is a legitimate human value that should be defended against the juggernaut of what we call progress, or whether that love is no more than reactionary nostalgia for a disintegrating past on the part of dominant groups to whom the familiar has been especially kind. To prevent too quick a jump to the latter charge, let me rephrase the question as follows. Do ways of life and their material expressions that are enjoyed by the many, or if by the few, then not at the expense of the many, deserve to be championed against what can seem to be the obliterating forces of time itself?

Certainly at one pole of the spectrum, erasures of the past are truly inevitable and so lie beyond the purview of critique. At this pole, valued thoughts, practices, and their material manifestations constantly "go under" almost of their own accord as one generation dies and another is born with what will become different tastes, sensibilities, and desires. Still, the organic process that Hegel summed up with the quip that the birth of the child spells the death of the parents means that history is as much an accretion of losses as it is an accretion of gains. Intellectual life is hardly exempt from this unfortunate rule. In my own field of political theory, for example, although canonical works continue to be revered, perhaps too revered, over many centuries, all sorts of elegantly turned and illuminating arguments and texts have fallen by the wayside as a result of nothing more insidious than the restless, or should we say heartless, movement of the human mind over time. I began Chapter 1 with W. B. Gallie's 1950s essay on essentially contested concepts partly to honor such half-buried but still suggestive lines of thought.

At the contingent and hence politically contestable end of the spectrum, erasures occur as a result of determined assaults on existing social habitats and habits by those who are able to amass the resources to launch such assaults and bring them to a successful conclusion. In the modern age, individuals who produce dramatic upheavals in the daily lives of others are most often not Machiavellian princes, emperors, or conquistadors but more ordinary human beings situated at key nodes of a structure of power so much larger and more complex than themselves that the assaults would continue regardless of whether any one of those human beings lived or died. As I intimated in my reference to olive groves above, one great culprit of such intentional yet impersonal demolitions have been modernizing projects undertaken by established states aspiring to greater wealth and power, including states to which movements for national self-determination have given birth. Whether modernizing states are ruled by dictators or democrats, and whether they are wedded to capitalism, industrial communism, or some strange amalgam of the two, they tend to exhibit an intense animus toward untamed landscapes, nomadic and rural existence, local knowledge, small-scale productive and market relations, vernacular architecture, "irrationally" ordered neighborhoods, material culture inherited from the past, and idiosyncratic or unpredictable thought and action at the grass roots level. As no scholar in the discipline of political science has done more to explore these effects of this animus than James C. Scott, I need only point interested readers to his life's work.[3]

The other great culprit implicated in the destruction of familiar landscapes and ways of life, to which I alluded in my reference to fences, is the capitalist compulsion towards infinite expansion in the pursuit of infinite profit. Like modernization, with which it is deeply entangled although not synonymous, capitalism relentlessly remakes the world in the name of development, advancement, and progress, but like the cases of republican-to-liberal democracy and ethnonationalism we examined in this book, it does so in the name of freedom as well, although the freedom of the individual rather than the demos or the ethnos. If its "progress" claim is highly debatable, its "freedom" claim is positively weird, as one of the most significant outcomes of capitalist development is the growth of mammoth concentrations of private power that dwarf the agency of any person and indeed surpass the clout of many sovereign states.

No critic of the domination effects of the capitalist "free market" can match the systematic rigor and acuity of Karl Marx, but on the question of capitalism's erasures of prior modes of production and the ways of life in which they were embedded, his habits of mind are less than fully satisfactory. To borrow Wendy Brown's metaphor of capital as a global sovereign that is "perpetual, absolute, and unifying" and "the source of all commands,"[4] Marx directs most of his scathing ire at *this* sovereign's rule to the exploitative capital/wage labor relation it "authorizes." He is less incensed by capital's acts of conquering non-capitalist environments and remolding them for capitalist use, although he is happy to sling barbs at bourgeois ideologies that romanticize those triumphs. Marx is hardly unaware of and in fact relishes in describing capitalism's destructive capacities—destructive not only vis-à-vis the pre-capitalist past but also vis-à-vis the capitalist-made present. However, his almost awestruck appreciation of capital's creative capacities and his belief in a historical dialectic lead him to anticipate a happy higher end to the whole destructive/creative process. Anyone who wishes to see the real uncolored by a teleological ideal will have to refuse to apply the term "progress" to the actualization of so-called objective historical ends. Anyone who wishes to see the real uncolored by bourgeois romanticism will have to reject the different notion that what happens in the future must be an ever-growing improvement over what happened in the past. That is, the critical realist must demote "progress" from a capital "P" concept that signifies either movement towards a grand historical telos or change as an automatic additive good-in-itself, to a lowercase "p" concept that signifies merely the degree to which any individual or collective actor has come closer to whatever goal that actor is trying to reach. After such a demotion, capitalism's onslaughts against ways of life incompatible with its own ethos and imperatives can slide into analytic view without those ways of life being branded by that token as "undeveloped," "regressive," or "backward."[5]

Its theory of history aside, Marxism is best known for disclosing the structural violence inherent in the capitalist/wage labor relation. However, there *are* minor chords in the tradition that convey the foundational violence, whether physical blows are used or not, by which capitalism defeats "foreign" modes of imagination, sentiment, and endeavor in the vicinity of its initial emergence, expands the geographical orbit of its sovereign power, and captures new arenas of practice in areas it already has "settled." One of those minor chords is struck by Marx himself in the closing section of the first volume of *Capital* on "the so-called primitive accumulation." Here he excoriates the methods by which land, raw materials, and labor-power were wrested from non-capitalist contexts to form the "first capital," those contexts disintegrating in that often bloody process.[6] An even fiercer condemnation of capitalism as a demolition project can be found in the last seven chapters of Rosa Luxemburg's *The Accumulation of Capital*, which detail capitalism's struggles against cooperative modes of productive life in pre-capitalist European peasant communities, in the small-scale stage of capitalist enterprise, and in non-capitalist countries colonized by the West.[7] In a respectively more literary and more historical vein, the British Marxists Raymond Williams and E. P. Thompson evoke the felt experience of loss, and the capacities, attachments, and outlooks of ordinary people that have since been lost to us, as a result of capitalist transformations of England that soon would radiate into the rest of the world.[8] Most recently, the Marxist geographer David Harvey has tracked new processes of "accumulation by dispossession" that increase capitalist profit by stripping away communally *and* individually enjoyed features of social life from developed and developing capitalist settings alike. Such processes include the privatization of formerly public goods from seeds and water to streets and ideas, the industrial depletion of the environmental commons, and the steamrolling over face-to-face relations of production and exchange by economic monoliths.[9] Although Harvey doesn't say it, those processes also include the sacrifice of private property in Hannah Arendt's sense of a secure home in the world for the many to the aim of increasing sheer quantitative wealth for the few. In sum, dispossession and erasure, which are here two sides of the same coin, constitute a key route to profit-making today. As Scott would add, this is a route that modernizing and modern states alike help to clear. In such a context, and as the June 2013 Taksim Square uprising in Turkey partly demonstrates, social movements to conserve material elements of a popularly enjoyed and habitable past against an imposed and asymmetrically rewarding future must be counted as a form of anti-sovereign politics, and a radical, not reactionary, form at that.

The political emancipation of wandering Jews

In his brilliantly offbeat *The Jewish Century*, Yuri Slezkine distinguishes between Apollonian and Mercurian social types, contrasting their different relationships to nineteenth-century nationalism and their opposite fates in the contemporary age. In pre- and early-modern societies, Apollonians (who, Slezkine jokes, turn into Dionysians when drunk) are majorities rooted in the land and attached to a set of venerated customs and traditions. They are parochial in outlook, robust in physique, agrarian or pastoral or military by occupation, suspicious of foreigners, hostile to cities, and angered by cosmopolitan mentalities. Conversely, Mercurians are itinerant exiles from other places and ethnic strangers where they happen to live. They are multilingual by necessity, urban by inclination, intellectually dexterous, and entrepreneurial as merchants and traders, with a talent for creating ideas and designing artifacts. My distinction in Chapter 1 between freedom as the ability to enjoy patterns of life to which one has grown attached and freedom as the ability to create something new is not unrelated to this Apollonian/Mercurian duality.

While diaspora populations are quintessential Mercurians, and while Jews were, before the birth of Israel, the quintessential diaspora group, Slezkine argues that processes of modernization press everyone to develop Mercurian traits in the long run. In the shorter run, however, nationalist movements compensate uprooted peasants by valorizing the ancient customs and rural culture of the nation, and they attack ethnic strangers for putatively undermining both. This potent mixture of valorization and attack put nineteenth-century European Jews, who were ethnic strangers in every nation-state, in a position even more unnerving than their also threatened or soon to be threatened analogues: the Indians in East Africa, the Lebanese in West Africa, the Chinese in South East Asia, the Parsis in India, the Armenians and Greeks moving back and forth between the Ottoman and Russian Empires.

As we have seen, Zionism proposed that Jews should stamp out their Mercurian virtues and re-fashion themselves as Apollonians by becoming peasants who could shoot in their own nation-state. Slezkine, however, reminds us of two other formidable answers to the Jewish Question. One was Russian communism, which attempted to transcend the alienation between Apollonians and Mercurians by blending the two types into one cosmopolitan yet popular mass. The other was American capitalism, which had turned Mercurianism into the ethos of a state and majority culture. Slezkine concludes that the American solution to the predicament of diasporic minorities proved more viable than the other two. Jews who had gravitated to Bolshevism with great internationalist passion and, as skilled Mercurians, rose to top positions in institutions from the Bolshoi to the Cheka became the target of purges after the Hitler–Stalin pact in 1939. The rise of Apollonian Russian nationalism in the 1940s, in combination with the Holocaust, greatly increased the appeal of Jewish nationalism to Russian Jews. But the Zionist alternative led the Jews who chose it from Mercurian strangeness "to a new kind of strangeness." It built an Apollonian polity based on "violent retribution" and "undiluted ethnic nationalism" just at the moment that the West was shedding Apollonianism for Mercurianism.[10] Although Slezkine doesn't say it, it was also just a moment before many Apollonians all over the world would metamorphose into Mercurians as a result of global capitalism's destructive and creative aspects; environmental crises; state collapse, civil wars, tyrannical rulers, corrupt elites, and other expressions of a general failure of political classes and institutions; and the shocks to the individual personality of such destabilizing turmoil.

Increasing numbers of "Jews" wander across the globe today—in the Palestinian case, as a direct result of the Zionist attempt to turn wandering Jews into Apollonians. The consequently outdated practice of hinging the political rights of individuals on their birth in a specific sovereign state territory or their exhibition of a specific sovereign people's blood type raises the question of how citizenship might be reconfigured so that people can exercise free political agency wherever they go and whoever they are, at least with respect to problems that affect them. Such a reconfiguration cannot be achieved simply by devising the right set of abstract laws and norms—as if in 1948, by the mere theoretical concoction of laws dictating the equal treatment of all individuals or of rules for conducting rational discourse between people with discordant perspectives, Jews and Arabs in Palestine could have been magically reconciled with one another. As Jabotinsky realized years ago, the anxiety-driven prejudices of natives towards foreigners (not to speak of the anxiety-driven prejudices of foreigners turned natives) is the far harder nut to crack, even and perhaps especially when the whole native/foreigner distinction has begun to break down. Neither can mere theoretical deconstructions of the nation vanquish the deeply felt solidarities and antipathies of those who see themselves as belonging to the same national group.[11]

There are, however, signs of progress, with a small "p," in the political emancipation of Mercurians, from the winning of rights for residents of certain Western cities to participate in local politics regardless of their national citizenship status, to the legalization of free movement of persons across national borders within the (admittedly still exclusive) European Union, to the fostering of social empathy and political identification across nation-state and ethnic boundaries by global communication technologies.[12] Even at the level of the sovereign state, there have always been examples of relatively hybrid and hybridity-welcoming citizen bodies, or at least there have been periods in which hybridity has been welcomed by them. Indeed, notwithstanding its original sin against Native Americans, the enslavement of Africans by its early landowning elites, the ongoing ambivalence of many of its citizens (including former immigrants) about foreigners arriving at its shores, and the desire of a (fortunately declining) number of Americans that it remain Christian and white, the United States itself is testimony that a polity can comprise heterogeneous peoples from elsewhere without disastrous after-effects. When Slezkine suggests that America is the best of the three answers to the Jewish Question, this is mostly why.

Natural freedom versus sovereign mastery of the earth

The tension between a preservationist ethos towards valuable aspects of the past and the footloose Mercurian social type can be fruitful rather than fatal if the Mercurians of the world learn to cultivate an Apollonian care for place, in distinction from a claim to sovereign power over national spaces. To explain why the care for place has become as critical to wellbeing in the twenty-first century as the individual right to political agency, let us take a brief detour through one of Patchen Markell's Arendtian-inflected arguments in *Bound by Recognition.*

Markell calls finitude a basic condition of human life, by which he means the vulnerability of every self to other selves as well as to the natural needs and mortal limitations of the body. The fact that finitude is ineliminable does not prevent people from trying to acquire sovereign power so that they can force others to "bear a disproportionate share" of vulnerability's costs and burdens.[13] Through class domination, for example, some selves shift the burden of sustaining their own biological life by exploiting the labor of others. Through democratic or ethnonational domination, as we have seen here, whole peoples can demand that others forfeit to them their familiar habitats.

Markell sees attempts to win freedom from finitude through sovereign invulnerability at the root of the refusal of dominant groups to recognize the equal humanity of those they have subjugated or marginalized. Subordinated groups that focus on the struggle for recognition of their identities and press sovereign states to enforce attitudes of "equal respect" for them may not merely misrecognize and help re-entrench the misrecognition of collective identities as essential and fixed. They also unwittingly may obscure the material interest in an unequal shouldering of the burdens of vulnerability that is the secret of much discursive cruelty, and that will not be corrected and may even be protected by reforms in how groups speak to and about one another. The Indian Treaty System and the Zionist struggle for Palestine in different ways illustrate Markell's point. The U.S. government's recognition of Indian tribes as sovereign nations served both as a veil over material asymmetries between settlers and indigenous groups and as a mechanism by which those asymmetries were worsened by legitimating "dispossession by consent." The Zionist project of turning the Jews into the majority people of Eretz-Israel required them to shift the burdens of minority vulnerability to Palestinian Arabs, with Jewish refusals of recognition to Palestinian Arabs the effect, not the cause, of that required shift.

There is, however, one search for sovereign freedom from finitude that does not give rise to struggles for recognition on the part of those forced to bear a disproportionate share of vulnerability's burdens and costs. However problematic Markell has proven such struggles to be, the absence of any opportunity for them is even more problematic, as this final case of sovereign freedom attests. This is the attempt of the human species to gain sovereign mastery over the earth so that it may vanquish all objects of aversion and manipulate everything else for the sake of satisfying human desires. The conceit that one element of nature can rise above the web of life in which it is embedded to achieve perfect freedom from that web is more delusional than any other type of attempt of a subject to free itself by becoming a king who can command others without their consent. In fantasy, the human species may be able to lift itself to a superior position outside and over the natural universe. In reality, regardless of how much scientists come to know about atoms, molecules, forces, gases, rays, genes, and planets, not one of them can ward off the effects on those atoms and planets of the actions of billions of human beings, or the boomerang effects on human beings of those effects.

The human ideal of mastering the earth (with mastering outer space as the next ambition) rests on a refusal to acknowledge the inevitable impacts of the natural world on the human species as an internal part of it, often although not always as a result of that part's interchanges with other parts. But that ideal also rests on a refusal of humans to recognize other elements of the natural world as values-in-themselves. Unfortunately—since winning recognition, for all its pitfalls, can be the first step towards pushing for more profound improvements— those elements are incapable of challenging refusals of recognition at the discursive level. Much more unfortunately, most life species are incapable of defending themselves physically against the actions of human beings as would-be earthly sovereigns. As the environmental effects of those actions multiply, every life species, including our own, will be at the mercy of natural processes with a far greater power to turn the world into "a desert and wasteland" than Vladimir Jabotinsky ever had.

Political theory is professionally preoccupied with political freedom, but at this moment in history a concept of what I will dub "natural freedom" needs to be elaborated and defended, too. This is the freedom to enjoy bodily life as one element of a non-dystopian universe, in which all species can exist at the level of, not bare life, but flourishing life. For our species, this means, quite banally, the freedom to breathe clear air, drink unpolluted water, and be outdoors without fear of catastrophic changes in the weather. But it also means the freedom to indulge in the sensory delights to be had in the physical world around us, including the delights of meeting natural life forms that are entrancing because they are neither like us nor for us.

How might the human species win the natural freedom described above, to the extent that it is still possible to win it? First, we would have to abandon delusions of sovereign mastery over the earth for a realistic view of ourselves as one especially potent element of nature in a relationship of delicate interdependence with all other elements, as well as cultivating an ethical view of other life species as having as fundamental a right to exist as we do (and a much more fundamental right than the "right" of any state to exist, given the artificial as opposed to organic nature of the state form). Second, we would have to acquire, very quickly, a far lighter ecological footprint on the earth than we have now. Third, as billions of people around the world already live at the lowest possible level of consumption for sustaining life, we would have to redistribute resources so that a lighter footprint would not be too painful for those billions to bear. With respect to recognizing these three requirements of natural freedom, indigenous movements around the globe have been in advance of the rest of us.

While we are so little masters of the earth that we cannot continue our way of life without destroying the conditions of even bare life for ourselves and other species, the changes that natural freedom demands are so drastic that it is impossible to conceive of their being made voluntarily, especially as they would severely curtail the freedom of the so-called sovereign individual. This makes it tempting to fantasize about a benevolent monarch with absolute power to impose earth-friendly rules of behavior on the entire human race. The clash between the free pursuit of desires as they are currently felt by many people across the globe and even the minimal conditions of natural freedom for all species of life puts ecological politics in a much bleaker position than the other forms of political resistance that are intimated by the thrust of this book. The struggle to preserve familiar practices and landscapes against powerful political and economic forces that would destroy them is ongoing, even if, given the complicity of global capital and modern or modernizing states, it is extremely difficult to wage or win. The struggle to secure the individual's political rights outside classic sovereign state parameters so that wandering minorities can enjoy political agency without having to become oppressive majorities is promising, although it has only just begun. More urgent than both, and less evidently the fruit of "more democracy" than either, the struggle to win natural freedom through a non-sovereign relation to the earth has the longest odds against it of all.

Still, even here there are surprises. If, against Herzl's earlier formulation, first there is, not the idea, but the context and crisis that provoke the idea, breakthroughs in thought can spark "miracles" of action that destabilize that context and create new openings for transcending that crisis. When breakthroughs in thought are addressed to a global audience, they have a chance to rattle thought and action on a universal scale. Thus, I hope I may be forgiven for concluding my remarks on the struggle for natural freedom, not with radical ecologists' visions of sustainable futures, and not with experimental paths to those futures that grassroots groups have tried to clear, but with an explicit assessment of the world's situation and an implicit call to action by the new Catholic Pope. Soon after his appointment, Francis denounced a global economic system "which tends to devour everything which stands in the way of increased profits ... whatever is fragile, like the environment, is defenseless before the interests of a deified market, which becomes the only rule."[14] Clearly, the spiritual leader of a global institution has no more power than any other individual to overturn that rule, and not only because he has no earthly coercive force at his disposal. But with respect to the reasons why *we* should contest the sovereign freedom of capital—and the sovereign freedom of every other self-aggrandizing force, for that matter—who has made the point more aptly, more fiercely, or with a more unexpected jolt to the reigning "common sense"?

Notes

Introduction

1   Hannah Arendt, *Men in Dark Times* (New York: Harcourt Brace Jovanovich, 1983 [1955]), 165. Benjamin's exact wording, as quoted by Arendt from his "Theses on the Philosophy of History," is "What we call progress is *this* storm."

2   For an argument on the increasingly antiquated nature of the idea of the industrial proletariat, see Guy Standing, *The Precariat: The New Dangerous Class* (London: Bloomsbury Academic, 2011).

3   James Tully, *Public Philosophy in a New Key*, vol. 1, *Democracy and Civic Freedom* (Cambridge: Cambridge University Press, 2008), 19, 25, 32.

4   William E. Connolly, *Pluralism* (Durham, NC: Duke University Press, 2005), 140.

5   Orlando Patterson traces what he calls sovereignal freedom or the idea of "freedom as total power" back to, in the non-Western world, the heretic Egyptian pharaoh Akhnaton in the fourteenth century BC; and back to, in the Western world, the fifth-century "aristocratic invitation [to all freeborn Greeks] to share in the overlordship of all slave peoples, that is to say, all non-Greeks." Orlando Patterson, *Freedom*, vol. 1, *Freedom in the Making of Western Culture* (New York: Basic Books, 1991), 38, 87. Patterson argues that sovereignal, personal, and civic freedom constitute a "three-chord" value in Western history, with the relative strength of each chord changing from ancient times through the Middle Ages to today. To translate my core argument, to the extent that it can be translated, into his terms: this book proposes that the idea of sovereignal freedom is as key as personal freedom to the modern age, and that new dangers emerge once sovereignal freedom is democratized. However, I read early modern theories of monarchical sovereign power as *not* applauding sovereignal freedom or the right of the monarch to do whatever he (or she) wants without limit or constraint, which those theories instead treat as the mark of tyranny. As for monarchical power in practice (as well as the actual

lower-level sovereignal powers of aristocrats and gentry)—it was
certainly capable of degenerating into such tyrannical forms, but it
was normally hemmed in by custom, constraining rituals, moral and
religious law, and prescribed obligations to inferiors (literal slaves
apart).

6   Karuna Mantena, "Another Realism: The Politics of Gandhian
     Nonviolence," *The American Political Science Review* 106, no. 2 (May
     2012): 455–70; 456.

7   Vladimir Jabotinsky, *The Story of the Jewish Legion*, ed. and trans.
     Samuel Katz (New York: Bernard Ackerman, 1945 [posthumous
     publication]), 178–9.

8   Patchen Markell, "The Rule of the People: Arendt, *Archê*, and
     Democracy," *American Political Science Review* 100, no. 1 (February
     2006): 1–14.

Chapter 1: The Sovereignty Concept

1   J. S. Mill, "On Liberty," in *John Stuart Mill: Three Essays*, ed. Richard
     Wollheim (Oxford: Oxford University Press, 1975 [1857]), 92.

2   See Elaine Scarry, *The Body in Pain* (Oxford: Oxford University Press,
     1985) for an analysis of war as a method in which wounded bodies
     are used to resolve ideational conflicts. On another note, these two
     notions of freedom clearly are similar in structure—it is the proper
     subject of freedom over which they mainly disagree. They also are
     equally dissimilar from other notions of what it means to be free, such
     as being neither a master nor a slave; being a creative subject, not a
     passive object, of history; being instinctually uninhibited; and being
     unburdened by the cares of the body and anxieties of the soul.

3   W. B. Gallie, "Essentially Contested Concepts," *Proceedings of the
     Aristotelian Society* 56 (1955–6): 167–98. Gallie sees conceptual
     open-endedness as a function of changing historical conditions, while
     I represent it as a function of a number of different factors, the first
     cited being the inherent restlessness of thought. For a discussion of
     the continued value of Gallie's insights for political science, see David
     Collier, Fernando Daniel Hidalgo and Andra Olivia Maciuceanu,

"Essentially Contested Concepts: Debates and Applications," *Journal of Political Ideologies* 11, no. 3 (October 2006): 211–46.

4   William E. Connolly, *The Terms of Political Discourse* (Lexington, MA: D. C. Heath, 1974).

5   Raymond Williams, *Marxism and Literature* (Oxford: Oxford University Press, 1977), 11–20.

6   See David Bollier, *Silent Theft: The Private Plunder of our Common Wealth* (New York: Routledge, 2003) for a forceful example of the critical value of these conceptual residues.

7   Quentin Skinner, *Liberty before Liberalism* (Cambridge: Cambridge University Press, 1998), 112.

8   Nicholas Greenwood Onuf, "Sovereignty: Outline of a Conceptual History," *Alternatives* 16 (1991): 425–46.

9   That political theorists tended to take "sovereignty" for granted by omission is exemplified in the absence of the term from even the index of Connolly's *The Terms of Political Discourse* when it was published in 1974, while 30 years later, in, for example, *Pluralism* (Durham, NC: Duke University Press, 2005) Connolly treated "sovereignty" as a highly significant problematic concept.

10   Hannah Arendt, *The Origins of Totalitarianism* (New York: Harcourt Brace, 1973 [1951]). Although very occasional references to national and popular sovereignty appear in the text, the term does not appear once in the index of *The Origins'* three volumes.

11   See Daniel Philpott, *Revolutions in Sovereignty: How Ideas Shaped Modern International Relations* (Princeton, NJ: Princeton University Press, 2001).

12   See, for example, Giorgio Agamben's left-Schmittian analysis of sovereign power as a "monarchical" decision over the life and death, not only of refugees and death-row prisoners who most obviously have been excluded from the protection of the law but also of the general citizen population, any of whose members are vulnerable to being demoted from inhabitants of political life to "bare life" by the sovereign power to declare the exception. Giorgio Agamben, *Homo Sacer: Sovereign Power and Bare Life*, trans. Daniel Heller-Roazen (Stanford, CA: Stanford University Press, 1998).

13   William E. Connolly makes a similar point when he criticizes

neo-Schmittian theorists who locate sovereign power in a "monarch" who decides the exception rather than in the interplay between state authority and the micropolitics of popular sentiments and inclinations. Sovereignty is thus not "he" but "*that* which decides an exception exists and how to decide it, with the *that* composed of a plurality of forces circulating through and under the positional sovereignty of the official circulating body." Connolly, *Pluralism*, 145. Yet Connolly seeks to save the value of sovereign power by showing us that it is always internally pluralistic, the result of a push and pull relationship between official sovereign authority and popular pressure, at both the domestic level and at the level of "global empire." My different argument is that, while actual sovereign power may be more the outcome of plural forces than the classical theory of sovereign power admits (even in the period of classic monarchical rule), the will to and project of sovereign power is inherently problematic.

14   Edmund Morgan, *Inventing the People: The Rise of Popular Sovereignty in England and America* (New York: W. W. Norton, 1988). For Morgan, while the rule of elites is inevitable, the ideal of popular sovereignty exposes that rule to legitimate democratic pressure.

15   For a critique of "emergency-think," even among democratic theorists, that legitimates sovereign decisionism and the state's suppression of popular political action by turning conflict into crises, see Bonnie Honig, *Emergency Politics: Paradox, Law, Democracy* (Princeton, NJ: Princeton University Press, 2011, 2009).

16   In her Agamben-inflected critique of Guantanamo Bay, Judith Butler analyses, in the wake of 9/11, the revitalization of monarchism as an assault on the separation of powers. In an "unchecked enlargement of executive power"(72), the law was suspended by the U.S. executive branch, which delegated to bureaucratic minions, or petty sovereigns, the power to keep terrorism suspects in "socially conditioned states of suspended life and suspended death" (67). Butler departs from Agamben in insisting that U.S. sovereign power abandoned very specific populations as opposed to the general citizen body. Still, by focusing on the executive decision to suspend the law by declaring an indefinite state of emergency, Butler downplays the role of "popular sovereignty" in the drama. The popular atmosphere of fear of terrorism and

anti-Muslim sentiment in the United States, which cannot be reduced to a mere product of government and media manipulation, surely helps explain the willingness of petty sovereigns to embrace their charge as well as the complacency of most citizens when details of torture in Guantanamo began to seep out. Judith Butler, "Indefinite Detention," in *Precarious Life: The Powers of Mourning and Violence* (London: Verso, 2006, 2004).

17 Saskia Sassen, *Losing Control? Sovereignty in an Age of Globalization* (New York: Columbia University Press, 1996). John Agnew, *Globalization and Sovereignty* (Lanham, MD: Rowman & Littlefield, 2009).

18 Michael Hardt and Antonio Negri, *Empire* (Cambridge, MA: Harvard University Press, 2000).

19 Wendy Brown, *Walled States, Waning Sovereignty* (New York: Zone Books, 2010), 64–5.

20 See "Perry Declares Texas' Rejection of Health Care Law 'Intrusions,'" *New York Times*, Tuesday July 10, 2012.

21 Brown, *Walled States*, 41.

22 Ibid., 104.

23 Ibid., 47.

24 Sigmund Freud, *The Future of an Illusion*, in *The Freud Reader*, ed. Peter Gay (New York: W. W. Norton, 1989 [1927]), 704.

25 Jean Bodin, *On Sovereignty: Four chapters from "The Six Books of the Commonwealth,"* ed. and trans. Julian H. Franklin (Cambridge: Cambridge University Press, 2006, 1992 [1576]), 38.

26 While Bodin posits the sovereign king as bowing to no higher sovereign power except God's, he alludes to a world of many sovereign princes, each superior to his subjects but equal among themselves. This is one reason he can contemplate the overthrow of a tyrant by a foreign prince but not one by the tyrant's subjects.

27 Bodin, *On Sovereignty*, 45, 4, 31.

28 Thomas Hobbes, *Leviathan*, ed. Richard Tuck (Cambridge: Cambridge University Press, 2005, 1996 [1651]), 117, 109.

29 Ibid., 9.

30 Ibid., 237.

31 Ibid., 135.

32   See Morgan, *Inventing the People*, for a historical rendering of this
     process in England and the United States.

33   Carl Schmitt, *Political Theology: Four Chapters on the Concept of
     Sovereignty*, trans. George Schwab (Chicago: University of Chicago, 2005
     [1922]).

34   As Orlando Patterson reminds us, there were earlier anticipations of
     the idea of popular sovereignty that were not, however, as politically
     influential, including the fourteenth-century theory of popular
     sovereignty elaborated by Marsilius of Padua. Tellingly, Patterson files
     such theories under his category of "civic freedom," not "sovereignal
     freedom." Patterson, *Freedom*, 389.

35   Jean-Jacques Rousseau, *The Social Contract or Principles of Political
     Right*, trans. Maurice Cranston (London: Penguin Classics, 1968 [1762]),
     51, 60, 61–2, 83.

36   Etienne Balibar, *We, the People of Europe? Reflections on Transnational
     Citizenship*, trans. James Swenson (Princeton, NJ: Princeton University
     Press, 2004), 148, 196.

37   Rousseau, *Social Contract*, 65.

38   Edmund Burke, *Reflections on the Revolution in France* in *Reflections
     on the Revolution in France and The Rights of Man* (New York: Anchor
     Books, 1973 [1790]), 140.

39   Hannah Arendt, "What is Freedom?" in Hannah Arendt, *Between Past
     and Future: Eight Exercises in Political Thought* (New York: Penguin,
     2006 [1961]), 162.

40   Ibid., 163.

41   Ibid., 147.

42   Ibid., 163.

43   The dismissal is unfair at least on the elitist score, given that Arendt uses
     "freedom" to capture not merely the glorious words and deeds of heroic
     individuals in the ancient world but also liberating breaks by ordinary
     people with entrenched institutions and practices at extraordinary
     moments in modern politics.

44   I hope it is plain that the enjoyment of whatever patterns of life are
     beloved is not the same thing as the stability of the particular political
     institutions that Arendt deems necessary to preserve a space for freedom
     in her "creating something new" sense of that term.

45 Heinz Lubasz, *The Development of the Modern State* (New York: MacMillan, 1964), 2–3.

46 Connolly, *Pluralism*, 140.

Chapter 2: Foundational Violence and the Politics of Erasure

1 On the covert mechanisms of violence at home and/or the overt expressions of violence abroad that have characterized Western liberal societies once they were established, Marxist, anti-colonial, and post-structural critics all have been loquacious, as has the less pigeonhole-able theorist of structural violence, Johan Galtung.

2 Augustine, *The Political Writings of St. Augustine*, ed. Henry Paolucci (South Bend, IN: Gateway, Henry Regnery, 1962), 16–17, from Augustine's *City of God*, XV [completed 427].

3 According to Augustine, even a universal earthly empire cannot avoid this crime, as its establishment would mean that one people lusting for dominance had acquired total power over the rest.

4 Friedrich Nietzsche, *On the Genealogy of Morals*, trans. Walter Kaufmann and R. J. Hollingdale (New York: Vintage Books, 1969 [1887]), 86–7.

5 Max Weber, "Politics as a Vocation," in *From Max Weber: Essays in Sociology*, ed. and trans. H. H. Gerth and C. Wright Mills (New York: Oxford University Press, 1958, 1946 [1919]), 78.

6 Jacques Derrida, "Force of Law: The 'Mystical Foundation of Authority,'" in *Acts of Religion*, ed. Gil Anidjar (New York: Routledge, 2002), 234, 242.

7 Ibid., 269.

8 Ibid., 270.

9 Hannah Arendt, *On Revolution* (New York: Penguin Classics, 2006 [1963]), 28–9.

10 Ibid., 169.

11 Ibid., 82.

12 Ibid.

13 Ibid., 158.

14   Ibid., 136.
15   Leo Strauss, *Natural Right and History* (Chicago: University of Chicago Press, 1965 [1950]), 1.
16   For an analysis of other implications of Arendt's performative reading of the "We hold," see Bonnie Honig, "Toward an Agonistic Feminism: Hannah Arendt and the Politics of Identity," in *Feminist Interpretations of Hannah Arendt*, ed. Bonnie Honig (University Park: Pennsylvania State University Press, 1995).
17   Arendt, *On Revolution*, 196.
18   Ibid., 206, 117.
19   Ibid., 110.
20   Ibid., 144.
21   Ibid., 175.
22   Ibid., 148, 156.
23   Ibid., 167.
24   Ibid., 164–5.
25   Ibid. 158–9.
26   For a detailed exploration of the diffuse character and fractured locus of sovereign power in the U.S. system of government, as well as for an overview of debates, not relevant to this book's focus, over where room for popular sovereign power lies in that country's liberal legal system, see Timothy A. Delaune, "Democratizing the Criminal: Jury Nullification as Exercise of Sovereign Discretion over the Friend-Enemy Distinction" (PhD diss., University of Massachusetts, Amherst, 2013).
27   James Madison, Alexander Hamilton, and John Jay, *The Federalist Papers*, ed. Isaac Kramnick (London: Penguin Classics, 1987 [1788]), 31.
28   Ibid., 91, 151.
29   Ibid., 155, 102, 103. For a historical account of Hamilton's special penchant for sovereign power concentration, which soon was to cause a rift between Madison and himself, see Stanley Elkins and Eric McKitrick, *The Age of Federalism: The Early American Republic, 1788-1800* (Oxford: Oxford University Press, 1993).
30   On allusions to Indians re trade, see Madison, *Federalist Papers*, 276–7 and *The Constitution*, reprinted therein, 493; re hostilities, see *Federalist Papers*, 96; re taxation and representation, see *The Constitution*, reprinted therein, 491.

31 Madison, *Federalist Papers*, 91. This is the passage that ends with the point we came across earlier, that this band "should never be split into a number of unsocial, jealous, and alien sovereignties."

32 Even John Pocock, in his magisterial rendering of the elements of thought that would crystallize in the founding of the American republic, writes as if the republic's fusion with its conceptual opposite, empire, occurred as a westward expansion into what had been a sheer unpopulated wilderness. The only hint Pocock gives of a native presence is in his occasional references to "wilderness savagery" as one of the two bad poles of early American possibility, the other bad pole being that of "metropolitan corruption." However, those references pertain most directly to settlers at the frontier, and only obliquely, and if obliquely, disparagingly, to an Indian presence. J. G. A. Pocock, *The Machiavellian Moment: Florentine Political Thought and the Atlantic Republican Tradition* (Princeton, NJ: Princeton University Press, 1975), Chapter XV. The various Straussian celebrations of the founding are even less inclined to acknowledge its violent destruction of Indian life. See, for example, Charles R. Kesler, ed., *Saving the Revolution: The Federalist Papers and the American Founding* (New York: Free Press, 1987). The rare references to Indians in this liberty-celebrating set of essays concern not the founding's implications for *their* liberty but the part the threat of their uprisings played in convincing voters in the states "of what they might gain from the existence of a national government." Edward C. Banfield, "Was the Founding an Accident?" in ibid., 272.

33 Obviously, not all recollection difficulties take the form of a total erasure from memory of the relevant situations and events, especially for generations not very far removed in time from them. For a study of the ways in which Indian leaders who fought to preserve their way of life were romanticized after the fact by those who had triumphed over them, see Gordon M. Sayre, *The Indian Chief as Tragic Hero: Native Resistance and the Literatures of America, from Moctezuma to Tecumseh* (Chapel Hill: University of North Carolina Press, 2005).

34 See, for example, Harry V. Jaffa, *How to Think about the American Revolution* (Durham: University of North Carolina Press, 1978). Jaffa argues that in embracing the natural law principle of political

equality, the American Revolution represented "the most radical break with tradition – with the tradition of Europe's feudal past – that the world had ever seen." In establishing a new government, the founders jettisoned all monarchical and aristocratic elements in favor of democratic republicanism and popular sovereignty, a principle that "has never been challenged within the American regime, by Conservatives any more than by Liberals or Radicals." Ibid., 16.

35   Francis Paul Prucha, *American Indian Treaties: The History of a Political Anomaly* (Berkeley: University of California Press, 1994), 130.

36   Pierre Clastres, *Society Against the State: The Leader as Servant and the Humane Uses of Power Among the Indians of the Americas*, trans. Robert Hurley (New York: Urizen Books, 1977, 1974), 20. Whether the indigenous taste for equality was extended to gender relations was another matter, but the "gender exception" to democracy was typical of the settlers, too. More relevant here is Clastres's representation of the Indian chief, as long as the tribe was not at war with outsiders, as someone who exercised power in an "anti-sovereign power" way, maintaining or restoring harmony in the group not by exerting a punitive authority that he in fact did not have but by persuading quarrelers to reconcile on the basis of "the strength of his prestige, his fairness, and his verbal ability," as well as his ongoing record of material generosity to group members. Ibid., 22.

37   Sandy Grande, *Red Pedagogy: Native American Social and Political Thought* (Lanham, MD: Rowman & Littlefield, 2004), 51.

38   Gordon S. Wood, *The Radicalism of the American Revolution* (New York: Alfred A. Knopf, 1991).

39   Stacy Kowtko, *Nature and the Environment in Pre-Columbian American Life* (Westport, CT: Greenwood Press, 2006), 129, 130, 131.

40   These are the arguments of, respectively, thinkers influenced by Edward Said's critique of orientalism, David E. Stannard, and all those who see racism as part of an essential white psychology. My approach to settler violence against indigenous populations accords more with Dustin Howes's analysis of "intersubjective violence" as "a matter of realizing oneself in the presence of others in ways that bring another's world crashing down on them." Dustin Howes, *Toward a Credible Pacifism* (Albany: State University of New York Press, 2009), 95.

41   David E. Stannard, *American Holocaust: The Conquest of the New World*
      (Oxford: Oxford University Press, 1992), 11.
42   Chief Justice Marshall, commenting in *Johnson v. M'Intosh (1823)*, as
      quoted in Wildenthal, *Native American Sovereignty on Trial*, 22.
43   Almost any treaty chosen at random from Charles J. Kappler, ed., *Indian
      Affairs: Laws and Treaties*, vol. 2, *Treaties* (Washington, DC: Government
      Printing Office, 1904), will display the same pattern as the following
      excerpts. From the Treaty with the Ottawa, Etc., 1821: "The Ottawa,
      Chippewa, and Pottawatamie Nations of Indians cede to the United States
      all the Land comprehended within the following boundaries: Beginning
      at a point on the south bank of the river St. Joseph of Lake Michigan ...
      and from the termination of the said line, following the boundaries of
      former cessions, to the main branch of the Grand River of Lake Michigan
      ... From the cession aforesaid, there shall be reserved, for the use of the
      Indians, the following Tracts." Ibid., 198-9. From the Treaty with the
      Creeks, 1825: "Whereas ... it is the policy and earnest wish of the General
      Government, that the several Indian tribes within the limits of any of
      the states of the Union should remove to territory to be designated on
      the west side of the Mississippi river, as well for the better protection and
      security of said tribes, and their improvement in civilization ... The Creek
      nation cede to the United States all the land lying within the boundaries
      of the State of Georgia ... It is further agreed between the contracting
      parties, that the United States will give, in exchange for the lands hereby
      acquired, the like quantity ... westward of the Mississippi [along with
      several hundred thousand dollars in the form of annuities]." Ibid.,
      214-15. From the Treaty with the Rogue River, 1853: "The Rogue River
      tribe of Indians do hereby cede and relinquish ... to the United States, all
      their right, title, interest, and claim to all the lands lying in that part of the
      Territory of Oregon, and bounded by lines designated as follows ... The
      United States agree to pay to the aforesaid tribe the sum of sixty thousand
      dollars, fifteen thousand of which sum to be retained ... to pay for the
      property of the whites destroyed by them during the late war." Ibid., 603.
44   This is one of the important insights to be gleaned from Vine Deloria Jr.
      and Raymond J. DeMallie's edited two volumes, *Documents of American
      Indian Diplomacy: Treaties, Agreements, and Conventions 1775-1979*
      (Norman: University of Oklahoma Press, 1999). The volumes also

improve upon Kappler in compiling agreements from 1871 through 1979 and including dialogues between Indians and whites especially in the Revolutionary period that record Indian voices, perspectives, philosophical outlooks, and rituals of friendship in the treaty process.

45   Dorothy V. Jones, *License for Empire: Colonialism by Treaty in Early America* (Chicago: University of Chicago Press, 1982), xi–xii. Jones argues that the Anglo-Indian treaty system had been one of "mutual compromise and accommodation" between independent parties, but by 1796 became a mechanism for Indian dispossession and white dominance through the transfer of "land from Indian ownership to ownership by the United States." Ibid., 186. For a fine-grained study of hybrid legal/political structures and mutual advantages of treaties in the colonial period, see Vicki Hsueh, *Hybrid Constitutions: Challenging Legacies of Law, Privilege, and Culture in Colonial America* (Durham, NC: Duke University Press, 2010). It is unclear whether Hsueh would find greater domination-effects in the later treaties signed by the tribes and a sovereign United States.

46   Prucha states that the British had paid for lands ceded by Indians rather than taking them by right of conquest, and the United States preferred that strategy, too, to avoid appearing as an oppressor. Prucha, *American Indian Treaties,* 54.

47   As quoted in Prucha, *American Indian Treaties*, 6. Stannard's Jefferson is even harsher: " '[I]f ever we are constrained to lift the hatchet against any tribe … we will never lay it down till that tribe is exterminated, or is driven beyond the Mississippi.' " The choice for the natives was either to be " 'extirpate[d] from the earth' or to remove themselves out of the Americans' way." Stannard, *American Holocaust*, 120.

48   Thus Chief Justice John Marshall asserted, in 1831, that to apply the English words " 'treaty' and 'nation' … to Indians as we have applied them to the other nations of the earth' " is to recognize the Indians as a " 'distinct political society, separated from others, capable of managing its own affairs and governing itself,' " and capable too of " 'being responsible … for any violation of their engagements.' " Prucha, *American Indian Treaties*, 4–5.

49   In an argument that complements mine, Eric Cheyfitz argues that English settlers symbolically converted the Indian relationship to place to fit within an English conceptual schema of sovereign possession, title,

and property, so that the land on which Indians lived could be alienated from them. This alienation could occur under two contradictory pretexts, one of which Cheyfitz notes and the other of which I do here. The first pretext is that, as the Indians did not "own" land they lived on, having neither fenced it in nor used their labor to increase its productivity for market exchange, that land could be claimed as private property by settlers, as if both Indians and settlers had endorsed the settlers' concept of place and bedrock rules for its habitation. The second pretext is that, as Indians "possessed" land in the English sense of the term (although collectively, not individually), Indian tribes could agree to exchange it for money, goods, or land elsewhere through treaties with the U.S. government. See Eric Cheyfitz, *The Poetics of Imperialism: Translation and Colonialism from "The Tempest" to "Tarzan"* (New York: Oxford University Press, 1991), esp. Chapter 3 and 59–60.

50 As we will see later, such a terrible irony has not prevented Indians and their allies from using the U.S.-Indian treaties, with their implicit recognition of American Indian sovereignty, as ammunition in the struggle for Indian rights to self-determination today. See, for example, Kevin Bruyneel, *The Third Space of Sovereignty: The Postcolonial Politics of U.S.—Indigenous Relations* (Minneapolis: University of Minnesota, 2007); David E. Wilkins, *American Indian Sovereignty and the U.S. Supreme Court: The Masking of Justice* (Austin: University of Texas Press, 1997); and David E. Wilkins and K. Tsianina Lomawaima, *Uneven Ground: American Indian Sovereignty and Federal Law* (Norman: University of Oklahoma Press, 2001).

51 Contemporary American Indian writers are divided on whether "sovereignty" is a European import or an essential feature of indigenous self-understanding, but, as we shall see, even those who do see it as indigenous interpret it in a way that emphasizes the right to autonomy, not mastery.

52 Prucha, *American Indian Treaties*, 4, 289.

53 For depressing historical corroboration of this truth, see Michael Mann, *The Dark Side of Democracy: Explaining Ethnic Cleansing* (Cambridge: Cambridge University Press, 2005).

54 Both Dale Turner and Taiaiake Alfred, whom we will look at in greater detail in a few moments, make this argument with respect to the Canadian

context, although the political conclusions they draw from it are quite
different. Alfred also notes that, even when it recognizes "Aboriginal title,"
the Canadian state always reserves its prerogative to use Indian lands
for industrial development, resource extraction, transportation, military,
business, and recreational access, for the "good" of "all Canadians."
Taiaiake Alfred, *Peace, Power, Righteousness: An Indigenous Manifesto*
(Don Mills, Ontario: Oxford University Press, 1999), 121.

55   William Cronon, *Changes in the Land: Indians, Colonists, and the
Ecology of New England* (New York: Hill and Wang, 1983), 79–80.

56   Ibid., 15.

57   For a rigorous analysis of contemporary indigenous politics with a focus
on the Mexican, not U.S. context; on entrenched structural injustice, not
the foundational violence by which one order supplants another; and on
movements that push for, not sovereign freedom, but democratic inclusion
in politics at the international, national, and local level, see Courtney Jung,
The Moral Force of Indigenous Politics: Critical Liberalism and the Zapatistas
(Cambridge: Cambridge University Press, 2008). Although I give far more
weight than Jung does to the human value of being able to sustain enjoyable
patterns of relations and practices as long as they *are* enjoyable, I agree with
both her repudiation of cultural essentialism (which is why I have avoided
boiling down "patterns of relations and practices" to "culture") and her
argument for a political standing for marginalized groups that "flows not
from who they are, but from what has been done to them." Ibid., 33.

58   John Sugden, *Tecumseh: A Life* (New York: Henry Holt, 1998), 9. For a
briefer account of the political impetus to and outcome of Tecumseh's
attempt to build a pan-Indian confederacy to resist white encroachment
on Indian lands, see R. David Edmonds, *Tecumseh and the Quest for
Indian Leadership*, 2nd ed. (New York: Pearson Longman, 2007).

59   Sugden, *Tecumseh*, 204–5.

60   James Tully has written extensively on the injustice of the sovereign
settler states in their dealings with first nations, the reasons why
indigenous populations cannot be considered ethnic minorities, and the
illegitimacy of their subjection to, in his case, Canadian law. However, he
follows three lines of thought at odds with the arguments of this chapter.

First, in contrasting the "bad" nineteenth-century Indian Acts
imposed on Aboriginal peoples "without their consent" with the "good"

seventeenth- through twentieth-century treaties between Aboriginal peoples and settlers, Tully claims that the treaty relationship has been the historic means by which "Aboriginal peoples and newcomer Canadians recognize each other as equal, coexisting and self-governing nations and govern their relations with each other by negotiations, based on procedures of reciprocity and consent." James Tully, *Public Philosophy in a New Key*, vol. 1, *Democracy and Civic Freedom* (Cambridge: Cambridge University Press, 2008), 226. I have argued, in contrast, that the treaty relationship was a mechanism by which the settler state expanded its sovereign authority over what had been Indian lands, with treaties functioning as non-directly violent instruments of sovereign state foundational violence. While Canadian treaty history may be less egregious than its U.S. counterpart, Tully admits elsewhere in the text that the extinction of Native land rights in Canada occurred both through conquest and "voluntarily (through treaties and cession)." Ibid., 263.

Second, Tully hinges the equality of Aboriginal peoples on the Canadian state's recognition of their sovereign status, thereby eliding the tremendous changes in *material* asymmetries that would have to occur for Aboriginal peoples to enjoy real sovereign power, not to speak of real equality with the non-native populations of North America. While he does press for a "leveling up" of the "appalling social and economic inequalities of Aboriginal peoples" (ibid., 247), his emphasis on the primacy of the politics of recognition sidesteps the way reciprocal recognition and respect can serve as both a substitute for material transformation and a discursive mystification of the deep material inequalities between so-called equal sovereign nations.

Third, Tully treats independence, autonomy, and self-governance as synonyms for sovereignty; suggests that sovereignty is a natural, not historically specific phenomenon when he speaks of "the sovereign nations that were already here" before the acquisition of sovereignty by the United States and Canada (ibid., 234); and does not remark on any clash between traditional indigenous philosophy and the ethos of sovereign power.

61 Cronon, *Changes in the Land*, 38.
62 Ibid., 62, 67. These features also seemed to characterize even those tribes that were more sedentary than the tribes Cronon mainly describes.

63   Alfred, *Peace, Power, Righteousness*, 22, 42, 42, 42.
64   Ibid., 55, 61, 62, 62.
65   Ibid., 59, 55–6.
66   Ibid., 52.
67   Dale Turner, *This is Not a Peace Pipe*, 67.
68   Ibid., 95.
69   Very weirdly, as John Sugden remarks in his biography of Tecumseh, the pro-Nazi Fritz Steuben churned out a series of popular Tecumseh novels in the 1930s representing the Indian chief as a führer who lost his war with the whites because Indians failed to unite under his leadership, the moral of his story being that Hitler would lose the war against his enemies if Germans did not unite under him. Sugden, *Tecumseh*, 393–4.
70   David Blackbourn, *The Conquest of Nature: Water, Landscape, and the Making of Modern Germany*, Chapter 5, "Race and Reclamation: National Socialism in Germany and Europe" (New York: W. W. Norton, 2006), 251–309.
71   Ibid., 273.
72   Hannah Arendt, *The Origins of Totalitarianism* (New York: Harcourt Brace, 1973 [1951]), 206.
73   Ibid., 191.
74   Alfred, *Peace, Power, Righteousness*, 63.
75   G. A. Cohen, "History, Ethics, and Marxism," in *Canadian Political Philosophy: Contemporary Reflections*, ed. Ronald Beiner and Wayne Norman (Oxford: Oxford University Press, 2001), 116.

Chapter 3: The Search for Sovereign Freedom

1   The United States at its very inception was guilty of other political sins as well, most obviously the sin of slavery. But the expansion of the sovereign power of the United States across the continent did not logically require the enslavement of Africans in the way that it required the dispossession of indigenous peoples.
2   It might be argued that the resolution of the U.N. General Assembly in November 1947 to partition British Palestine into a Jewish and an Arab state provided a prior, higher right – at least in the legal sense of the term

"right" – of the Jews to just over half of Mandatory Palestine. But whether the U.N. decision itself was grounded in a prior, higher *moral* right was hotly contested by both parties. The Arabs rejected the partition plan for turning them from a majority into a minority on one side of the partition line. Although supporting partition in the short term, the Zionist leadership disagreed with the plan's geographical limits on the Jews.

3   For the differences between the religious Old and the colonizing New *Yishuv*, as well as differences between "practical" and "political" Zionism (the former less practical in the political sense of the term than the latter, from the latter's point of view), and also for the distinctive mentalities of each wave of Jewish immigrants to Palestine, see Walter Laqueur, *A History of Zionism* (New York: Schocken Books, 1976, 1972), esp. Chapter 6, and David Vital, *The Origins of Zionism* (Oxford: Clarendon Press, 1980, 1975).

4   J. C. Hurewitz, *The Struggle for Palestine* (New York: W. W. Norton, 1950). Hurewitz reports that after an increase in Jewish immigration for religious reasons in the first half of the nineteenth century, as a result of persecution the number of Jews in Palestine grew "from 12,000 in 1845, and 47,000 in 1895, to nearly 85,000 in 1914." After declining in 1919 to 65,000 or 10 percent of the total population, by 1936 the Jewish population had reached, through new influxes, almost 30 percent of the total population. Ibid., 27.

5   Yosef Gorny, *From Binational Society to Jewish State: Federal Concepts in Zionist Political Thought, 1920–1990, and the Jewish People* (Leiden, The Netherlands: Brill, 2006), 171–2. Gorny tracks the various federal and confederal ideas that surfaced in Zionist debates in this 70-year period, displaying a "utopian" strain of Zionist thought on the co-existence of peoples in the Middle East that eventually gave way to realism on both the left and the right.

6   As David Ben-Gurion remarked to his Labor Party's Central Committee in 1949, "'Land with Arabs on it and land without Arabs on it are two very different types of land,'" and although there were arguments about whether it was better to try to gain less land with fewer Arabs or more land with more Arabs, it was as much land as possible with as few Arabs as possible that was for almost all the ideal. Tom Segev, *1949: The First Israelis* (New York: Henry Holt, 1998, 1986), 28.

7   Frantz Fanon, *The Wretched of the Earth*, trans. Constance Farrington
    (New York: Grove Weidenfeld, 1991 [1963]), 35. Of course, Fanon was
    addressing this replacement in the context of decolonization.

8   This is the position that Maxime Rodinson takes when, dismissing
    "both the intemperate idealization of the movement by Zionists and
    their sympathizers and the no less frenzied 'diabolization' in which their
    opponents have often indulged," he finds in Zionism "all the unpleasant
    features of nationalism, beginning with contempt for the rights of
    others." Maxime Rodinson, *Cult, Ghetto, and State: The Persistence of the
    Jewish Question* (London: Al Saqi Books, 1983), 150-1.

9   Quoted in Bennie Morris, *Righteous Victims: A History of the
    Zionist-Arab Conflict, 1881-1999* (New York: Alfred A. Knopf, 1999),
    49, 38.

10 Ibid., 37-8.

11 Ahad Ha-Am, "The Jewish State and the Jewish Problem" (1897), in *The
    Zionist Idea*, ed. Arthur Hertzberg (New York: Atheneum Macmillan,
    1969, 1959), 268.

12 Quoted in Morris, *Righteous Victims*, 47-8. Morris is, however, alert to
    complexities with respect to how the sense of superiority and disdain
    surfaced in relations between Arabs and Jews. He notes that Jews had
    flourished at some junctures in Islamic societies, especially between
    850-1250, but generally were seen as second-class citizens by Islam,
    often humiliated and sometimes persecuted even before the emergence
    of Zionism. The fact that Muslims traditionally viewed Jews as inferior
    weaklings made their assent to sovereign mastery in Israel all the more
    cause for anger and resentment. Conversely, some early Israeli leaders
    were as astute as Ha-Am about the psychological complexities of the
    master/slave relationship on the Jewish side. Segev quotes Pinhas
    Lavon, General Secretary of the national labor union, *Histadrut*, as
    warning in 1948 of the obstacles to " 'Jewish–Arab co-existence' "
    posed by the " 'Israeli-born generation, with its crude and primitive
    nationalism,' " and " 'the Oriental communities, with their historical
    and natural urge to avenge the years of humiliation and repression they
    suffered in Arab countries, which could easily be aroused when they
    suddenly discover that now we are the masters.' " Segev, *1949: The First
    Israelis*, 46.

13 Evoking the self-mastery that becoming a sovereign self demands, David Ben-Gurion later would call the diaspora type of Jew " 'the debris of Jewish humanity' " that had to be melted down and reconstituted into a " 'new human type,' " with the capacity for " 'Independence and national freedom.' " Quoted in Segev, *1949: The First Israelis*, 292–3. For an analysis of how this self-domination required the erasure of two millennia of the Jewish past, and how that erasure was used to enhance the sovereign power of the Jewish state, see Idith Zertal, "From the People's Hall to the Wailing Wall: A Study in Memory, Fear, and War," in *Representations* 69 (Winter 2000): 96–126.

14 For an analysis of the Jewish-only labor principle that emphasizes the second motive of labor Zionism noted above, as well as the consistency with which ethnonationalism trumped socialist principles at every turn, see Zachary Lockman, "Land, Labor and the Logic of Zionism: A Critical Engagement with Gershon Shafir," in "Past is Present: Settler Colonialism in Palestine," special issue, *Settler Colonial Studies* 2, no. 1 (2012): 9–38.

15 Segev, *1949: The First Israelis*, 69–79. Segev puts the figure of immigrants taking over Palestinian houses at between 140,000 and 160,000.

16 Ibid., 46. The lower figure for the number of refugees is Segev's; the higher is Rashid Khalidi's in his *The Iron Cage: The Story of the Palestinian Struggle for Statehood* (Boston: Beacon Press, 2006), 189. For a study of the Palestinians who remained in Israel, see Ian Lustick, *Arabs in the Jewish State: Israel's Control of a National Minority* (Austin: University of Texas, 1980).

17 Segev, *1949: The First Israelis*, 80–4. Segev also reports that military officials used their authority to expel villagers from their homes, preventing them from working their land, which the Minister of Agriculture then declared uncultivated and handed over to Jews to farm without a title. For a detailed investigation of the Israeli erasure not only of Palestinian places but also of the very names of those places on the map of Israel, see Meron Benvenisti, *Sacred Landscape: The Buried History of the Holy Land since 1948*, trans. Maxine Kaufman-Lacusta (Berkeley: University of California Press, 2000). For an investigation of the participation of Israel archaeology in the erasure process, see Nadia Abu El-Haj, *Facts on the Ground: Archaeological Practice and Territorial*

Self-Fashioning in Israeli Society (Chicago: University of Chicago Press, 2001).

18   For a recent example of "good/bad" splitting between the pre- and post-1967 period, see David Remnick, "The Party Faithful," *New Yorker*, January 21, 2013, 38–49.

19   While David Ben-Gurion does not figure in this study, see Shabtai Teveth, *Ben-Gurion and the Palestinian Arabs: From Peace to War* (Oxford: Oxford University Press, 1985) for an account of his initial thoughtlessness about Palestinian Arabs, his later attempts to square the circle of Jewish self-determination and Arab rights in Palestine as well as of ethnonational segregation and democratic socialist labor principles, and the morphing of his early insistence that Jewish sovereign freedom requires justice into his embrace of domination as the route to Jewish sovereign power. Teveth, however, asserts that the difference between Ben-Gurion and Jabotinsky on the subject of Jewish–Palestinian Arab affairs was always one of tactics and strategy, not ultimate goals, with Ben-Gurion's seeing bi-national autonomy and partition simply as necessary stepping-stones en route to a completely Jewish Palestine.

20   For a detailed study of the Revisionist Right and Jabotinsky's role in it, see Yaacov Shavit, *Jabotinsky and the Revisionist Movement 1925–1948* (London: Frank Cass, 1988).

21   Neve Gordon, *Israel's Occupation* (Berkeley: University of California Press, 2008), 5–6. Only about 17,000 out of the 120,000 who applied were eventually allowed to return. Morris puts the numbers at 200–250,000 Arabs fleeing, driven from, or enticed to leave the West Bank, 70,000 from Gaza, and 80–90,000 from the Golan Heights. Morris, *Righteous Victims*, 328.

22   Jeff Halper, *An Israeli in Palestine: Resisting Dispossession, Redeeming Israel* (London: Pluto Press, 2010, 2008), 33.

23   Morris put the number of this remnant in 1967 at 400,000. Morris, *Righteous Victims*, 336.

24   Israel's most recent twist on the solution to this conundrum has been to shrink the areas of Palestinian habitation to their smallest possible extent, take as much land and other natural resources as possible for Jewish settlement and use, unload the management of everyday life in non-contiguous Palestinian "population centers" to Palestinian

authorities, and retain sovereign security control over the relationship between those centers, Israel, and the outside world.

25 Halper, *Israeli in Palestine*, 301.

26 Gordon, *Israel's Occupation*, 204. Gordon reports that house demolitions in the first four years of the second Intifada left more than 24,000 Palestinians homeless.

27 Halper, *Israeli in Palestine*, 41–4, and Appendix 1, 301. Halper, who derived his estimates mainly from United Nations figures, estimates that only 5 percent of house demolitions in the Occupied Territories served legitimate security purposes.

28 Quoted in ibid., 43.

29 Gordon, *Israel's Occupation*, 193–4. Israel Shahak and Norton Mezvinsky give the figure of 100,000 Jewish settlers in the West Bank, Gaza, and the Golan Heights in 1999, with another 250,000 in "Greater Jerusalem." Israel Shahak and Norton Mezvinsky, *Jewish Fundamentalism in Israel*, new ed. (London: Pluto Press, 2004), 78.

30 Israel has established "about 250 Jewish settlements in the West Bank and East Jerusalem since 1967." Nick Cumming-Bruce and Isabel Kershner, "U.N. Panel Sees Violations in Israeli Settlement Policy," *New York Times*, Febuary 1, 2013.

31 *National Public Radio* Evening News, March 19, 2013.

32 Eyal Weizman, *Hollow Land: Israel's Architecture of Occupation* (London: Verso, 2007), 116–18. This was in addition to new land in the Occupied Territories acquired through private purchase contracts. Land expropriated by the state on security grounds increased greatly after 2001 with the building of the separation wall, which Gordon estimates would, when completed, sweep 12 percent of Palestinian land into the space between the wall and the pre-1967 borders of Israel. Gordon, *Israel's Occupation*, 213. Meanwhile, planning regulations have been used to establish Jewish hegemony over the whole of Jerusalem, with the municipality issuing, from 1967 to 2007, "an annual average of 1500 building permits to Jewish Israelis" and constructing "90,000 housing units for Jews in all parts of East Jerusalem," while limiting Palestinian permits to an average of 100 a year, imposing lower height levels on Palestinian houses, and declaring many existing Palestinian structures illegal. Weizman, *Hollow Land*, 49. According to a 2013 report in *The*

Economist, "in the past 45 years of Israeli occupation the army has redistributed around 70% of the West Bank land designated as state-owned either to Jewish settlers or to the World Zionist Organization, whereas less than 1% of supposedly state-owned land was granted to Palestinians." "The Palestinians' West Bank: Squeeze Them Out," *Economist*, May 4, 2013.

33 Weizman, *Hollow Land*, 147.

34 Chaim Levinson, "Israel introduces 'Palestinian only' bus lines, following complaints from Jewish settlers," *Haaretz Digital Editions*, Friday April 12, 2013. (Levinson's original posting, March 3, 2013, reports the decision of an Israeli bus company to operate separate lines for Palestinians and Jews from the West Bank to central Israel.)

35 David Lloyd, "Settler Colonialism and the State of Exception: The Example of Palestine/Israel," in "Past is Present: Settler Colonialism in Palestine," special issue, *Settler Colonial Studies* 2, no. 1 (2012): 59–80.

36 See, for example, Jodi Rudoren, "Some Fear a Soccer Team's Racist Fans Hold a Mirror Up to Israel," *New York Times*, January 31, 2013. This news report describes a banner calling for racial purity by fans and members of the Beitar Jerusalem team in Israel, in protest of the team owner's attempt to recruit two Muslim players from Chechnya; the story also notes an incident in March 2012, in which hundreds of Beitar's fans "stormed a mall near the stadium" to beat up Arab workers. For a detailed study of the fundamentalist religious right in Israel and its attitudes towards Arabs as Gentiles, see Shahak and Mezvinsky, *Jewish Fundamentalism in Israel*, especially Chapters 1 and 6. See Gordon, *Israel's Occupation*, on state-sanctioned settler violence, 140–3.

37 Sometimes the lesson was learned quite self-consciously, as in the 1930s, when the Zionist underground organization Irgun received military training from the Polish army and pro-Mussolini Zionist navel cadets received training from the Italian fascist military. See Eran Kaplan, *The Jewish Radical Right: Revisionist Zionism and its Ideological Legacy* (Madison, WI: University of Wisconsin Press, 2005).

38 For a vivid evocation of multicultural life in Salonica under the Ottomans and its disintegration after the rise of nationalism, see Mark Mazower, *Salonica, City of Ghosts: Christians, Muslims and Jews 1430–1950* (New York: Alfred A. Knopf, 2005).

39 In his introduction to *The Zionist Idea*, Arthur Herzberg describes the dawning realization of Jews that liberal and "tribal" nationalisms were not "French" versus "Teutonic" or characteristic of different countries but were different strains running through every country in Europe (46). Two of our illustrative Zionists go further than Herzberg, suggesting that under the veneer of even the most enlightened strain of European nationalism lurked the chauvinistic form.

40 International socialism stood apart in offering outsiders, including the Jews, a cosmopolitan political community in opposition to the nation-state, but while the socialist movement repudiated racial, ethnic, and ethnonational divisions at the theoretical level, it failed at the practical level to pay those divisions the attention they deserved.

41 *Israeli Declaration of Independence*, 1948.

42 In a double irony, that imperative was heightened from 1948 onwards with every new Arab attack on the Jewish state, which most Jews misrecognized as eternal anti-Semitism instead of anti-Western, anti-colonial animus; while each new attack on diasporic Jewish communities in the name of anti-Zionism that could legitimately be called anti-Semitic triggered a new mini-*Aliyah*.

43 Can every relation of domination and subjection be accurately filed under the master/slave rubric? Sharon R. Krouse, in her own critique of sovereign freedom, intimates that that rubric should be reserved for relations of labor exploitation, asserting that some forms of oppression, such as the oppression of homosexuals (and, by extension, Jews and other minorities), resemble the bars of imprisonment more than the chains of slavery. Sharon Krouse, "Freedom Beyond Sovereignty," politicalscience.stanford.edu/Workshops/Political Theory Workshop/ Sharon Krouse (March 9, 2012). To be sure, "mastery and servitude" is more metaphorical than literal when groups are disempowered via marginalization than when they are used as chattel labor. Nevertheless, the majority ethnic/religious/national group in a society can be called the "master" of that society *vis-à-vis* the minorities it marginalizes, especially in light of the material and psychological rewards to be gained from belittling, persecuting, and/or dispossessing weaker social groups.

44 While some feminists have borrowed for themselves the trope of the self who attains sovereign freedom through transcending the master/

slave relationship, I see sovereign power and hence sovereign freedom as more a masculine than either a feminine or a feminist fantasy and so have taken the liberty of using the masculine subject form here.

45 Mezvinsky has something of this unconscious desire in mind when he writes in his preface to the new edition of *Jewish Fundamentalism* that "many Israeli Jews are chauvinists who feel pride in the display of Jewish power [in the context of the passage, over Palestinians] and considered it to be compensation for centuries of Jewish humiliation." Ibid., vii.

46 Albert Memmi, *The Liberation of the Jew*, trans. Judy Hyun (New York: Viking, 1973 [1966]), 27.

47 Vladamir Jabotinsky, "Amen," *The Jewish Herald*, July 21, 1939, excerpted in *Political and Social Philosophy*, 40. Further in the same piece, Jabotinsky writes that "the worst of all horrors known to history is called *galuth*, dispersion; and the blackest of all characteristics of *galuth* is the tradition of the cheapness of Jewish blood, on the spilling of which there is no prohibition and for which you do not pay. To this an end has been made in Palestine." Ibid., 40–1.

48 Albert Memmi, *Decolonization and the Decolonized*, trans. Robert Bononno (Minneapolis: University of Minnesota Press, 2006, 2004), 45. Memmi makes this point in a book that bluntly indicts Third World societies for the impoverishment of their peoples and their continued exposure to violence half a century after their independence from colonial rule, as a result of tyrannical native leaders, corrupt elites, supine intellectuals, and power-hungry fundamentalist sects.

49 There were precedents, however. For an account of and excerpts from their works, see Hertzberg, *Zionist Idea* and Laqueur, *History of Zionism*, Chapter 2.

50 Illustrating the diasporic condition of the Jews that Zionists intended to cure, *The Jewish State* was translated during Herzl's lifetime into Russian, Hebrew, English, Yiddish, Romanian, Bulgarian, French, and German with Hebrew characters. Vital, *Origins of Zionism*, 260.

51 For Herzl's attempts to sway world leaders, see John C. G. Rohl, "Herzl and Kaiser Wilhelm II: A German Protectorate in Palestine?" and Edward Timms, "Ambassador Herzl and the Blueprint for a Modern State," in *Theodor Herzl and the Origins of Zionism*, ed. Ritchie

Robertson and Edward Timms (Edinburgh: Edinburgh University Press, 1997), 27–38 and 12–26.

52 For an engaging narrative of his agitation for a Jewish Legion in the British Army in World War I, which also reveals his mixture of disdain and respect for the British upper class and the Jewish working class in Britain, as well as his unmixed contempt for the Turks and Jewish assimilationists, see Vladimir Jabotinsky, *The Story of the Jewish Legion*, ed. and trans. Samuel Katz (New York: Bernard Ackerman, 1945). Joseph B. Schechtman, Jabotinsky's close political ally and biographer, also notes that Jabotinsky was a devoted father figure to the Religious Revisionists and the *Irgun*, the clandestine military organization engaged in armed reprisals against the Arabs and the British. Joseph B. Schechtman, *The Life and Times of Jabotinsky*, vol. 2, *Fighter and Prophet: The Last Years* (Silver Springs, MD: Eshel Books, 1986, 1961), 405–91.

53 Albert Memmi, *Jews and Arabs*, trans. Eleanor Levieux (Chicago: J. Philip O'Hara, 1975), 73.

54 In that last book, which broke with his earlier, empathetic descriptions of Arab societies, Memmi exclaims: "*Jewish Arabs*—that's what we would have liked to be, and if we have given up the idea, it is because for centuries the Moslem Arabs have scornfully, cruelly, and systematically prevented us from carrying it out." Ibid., 20.

55 Ibid., 95.

56 Theodor Herzl, *The Diaries of Theodor Herzl*, ed. and trans. Marvin Lowenthal (New York: Dial Press, 1956 [from a 1896 entry]), 199.

57 For a more detailed analysis of Jabotinsky's philosophy and its aesthetic dimensions, see Kaplan, *Jewish Radical Right*.

58 Vladimir Jabotinsky, "Sippur Yamai," *Autobiography*, excerpted in *Political and Social Philosophy*, 48.

59 Vladimir Jabotinsky, "On State and Social Problems," in *From the Pen of Jabotinsky* (Capetown, South Africa: Unie-Volkspers BPK, 1941), 64.

60 Vladimir Jabotinsky, *Prelude to Delilah*, excerpted in *Political and Social Philosophy*, 38.

61 Vladimir Jabotinsky, "The Ideology of the Betar," in *From the Pen of Jabotinsky*, 49.

62 Valdimir Jabotinsky, "The Ideology of Betar," (1934), excerpted in *Political and Social Philosophy*, 126–7. My edition of *From the Pen of*

Jabotinsky, from which "The Ideology of the Betar" is reproduced, does not have this precise line in it; the translation as a whole of my edition is less vivid than that of the Sarig ed., Feder trans. text.

63   "The woman" appears in Memmi's list of dominated "men" that also includes the Jew, the worker, the colonized, and the Negro, but Memmi's views on women have been checkered. For example, he complained in a late interview of the sexual temptations for men of women who are covered and women who are skimpily dressed, women's veils tempting men to tear them off to see what delights they are hiding, and women's short skirts tempting men to tear them off because those delights are already half exposed. Gary Wilder, "Irreconcilable Differences: A Conversation with Albert Memmi," *Transition*, Issue 71 (1996): 158–77.

64   Theodor Herzl, *Altneuland*, trans. Paula Arnold (Haifa: Haifa Publishing, 1960 [1902]), 94. Of course, the fact that Herzl constructed a character with such sentiments could be taken as evidence that he was worried at some level about how the indigenous Palestinian population would respond to Zionism's impact. He also made a more sinister comment in his diaries, which Morris reports from a June 12, 1895 entry, of the need for a "gentle" expropriation of poor Arabs and their removal from the territory of the Jewish state. Morris, *Righteous Victims*, 21–2.

65   Jabotinsky also did not hesitate to prescribe the Jews' self-domination by means of disciplinary training to transform the defenseless, ill-mannered, and pallid ghetto Jew into a muscular, proud, victorious type evoking the ideal of the "Aryan." For more on this score, see Michael Stanislawski, *Zionism and the Fin de Siècle: Cosmopolitanism and Nationalism from Nordau to Jabotinsky* (Berkeley: University of California Press, 2001).

66   Memmi, *Liberation of the Jew*, 287, 289, 292.

67   Ibid., 288.

68   Memmi, *Jews and Arabs*, 216.

69   Theodor Herzl, *Zionist Writings: Essays and Addresses*, vol. 2, *August, 1898–May, 1904*, trans. Harry Zohn (New York: Herzl Press, 1975 [from a 1901 entry]), 173. Alex Bein, in a short biographical essay at the front of *The Jewish State*, quotes Herzl as writing in his diary, "'The state exists as essence in the will-to-the-state of a people, yes, even in that will in a

single powerful person … The territory is only the concrete basis, and the state itself, with a territory beneath it, is still in the nature of an abstract thing … In Basle I created the abstraction, which, as such, is invisible to the great majority.'" Herzl, *Jewish State*, 53.

70 "I believe that pure ideological activity is likely to be as constructive as work which creates 'real' things such as houses and colonies … The ideological constructive factor is more important and longer lasting than the material-constructive one." Vladimir Jabotinsky, "Etliche Brief Copien," *Der Moment*, 8 April, 1934, excerpted in *Political and Social Philosophy*, 14.

71 Vladimir Jabotinsky, *The Jewish War Front* (London: George Allen & Unwin, 1940), 63, 29–30.

72 Historians have disputed Herzl's account of his politicization by the Dreyfus Affair, but what is not in dispute is the fact that his Zionist sympathies crystallized over the course of the affair, which by 1897 had persuaded him of the grave problem that European Jews were up against. For an account of that dispute and indeed for a supple study of Herzl, Jabotinsky, and other Zionists against the backdrop of European intellectual life at the turn of the century, see Stanislawski, *Zionism and the Fin de Siècle*.

73 Theodor Herzl, "The Situation in France," *Die Welt*, December 24, 1897, in Theodor Herzl, *Zionist Writings: Essays and Addresses*, vol. 1, *January 1896–June 1898*, trans. Harry Zohn (New York: The Herzl Press, 1973), 198, 200.

74 Herzl, *Jewish State*, 136–8.

75 Hannah Arendt, "The Jewish State: Fifty Years After: *Where Have Herzl's Politics Led?* (May 1946), in *The Jew as Pariah: Jewish Identity and Politics in the Modern Age*, ed. Ron H. Feldman (New York: Grove Press, 1978), 171, 166. Arendt moreover sees Herzl's prescriptions for a Jewish state as fraught with danger for both Jews and Arabs, and she is scathing about the way Zionists turned those prescriptions into practice. See Hannah Arendt, "Zionism Reconsidered" (October 1944), in ibid., 131–63.

76 Herzl, *Jewish State*, 89.

77 Theodor Herzl, "Opening Address at the Second Zionist Congress" (August 28, 1898) in *Zionist Writings*, vol. 2, 15.

78   As Jabotinsky put the last point, "When the nation requires an authentic
     creation in Russian, they will reject the work of the alien and state: the
     imitation is admirable and perhaps better than the Russian creation; but
     pardon me, we require a genuine Russian creation." Vladimir Jabotinsky,
     "On the Wrong Road," *Diaspora and Assimilation*, excerpted in *Political
     and Social Philosophy*, 139.

79   Jabotinsky, *Jewish War Front*, 108.

80   Jabotinsky, "The Ideology of Betar," excerpted in *Political and Social
     Philosophy*, 79. Sarig notes this line as coming from this essay in *From
     the Pen of Jabotinsky*, but without a page number in the citation. My
     edition of that text does not have this precise line in it, although it less
     vividly articulates the same sentiment.

81   As Jabotinsky noted, "Had there been no Jews in Poland," there would
     still have been competition, but "the 'crusade' … would have assumed a
     less concentrated form, a struggle of 'all against all.'" Jabotinsky, *Jewish
     War Front*, 78.

82   Ibid., 38.

83   Ibid., 105.

84   Herzl, *Altneuland*, 189. On their experience of the warmth of the
     Jewish community, our three Zionists seem to differ greatly. In his
     autobiographical novels, Memmi evokes a picture of the traditional and
     sometimes claustrophobic Jewish world in which he was enveloped in
     Tunisia, although his success in school provided him with a ticket out.
     The more affluent and deracinated Herzl and Jabotinsky seemed to
     romanticize that warmth from the standpoint of outsiders looking in
     during a fierce storm on a cozy domestic hearth.

85   Theodor Herzl, "Letter to the *Berliner Tageblatt*, January 4, 1898," in
     Zionist Writings, vol. 1, 208–9.

86   Theodor Herzl, "Opening Address at the Fourth Zionist Congress,
     August 13, 1900," in *Zionist Writings*, vol. 2, 152.

87   Theodor Herzl, "For a Jewish State," Address to the Maccabean Club,
     London, July 6, 1896, in *Zionist Writings*, vol. 1, 38. Even Jews seeking
     refuge from national chauvinism in international socialism would be
     "sloughed off" when socialism becomes "saturated with Jews." Theodor
     Herzl, "The Social Democrats and the Jewish Question," June 17, 1897,
     in ibid., 86–7.

88 Jabotinsky, *Jewish War Front*, 135. Jabotinsky's exact words are "The Jewish tramp is not wanted."

89 Ibid., 62, 36, 62, 62, 74.

90 Theodor Herzl, "Sir Francis Montefiore," *Die Welt*, February 17, 1899, in *Zionist Writings*, vol. 2, 61. Actually, Herzl was speaking specifically about the great Jewish philanthropists, but at least with respect to the "Politics, Poor" score, his indictment of Jewish political inexperience is more general.

91 Vladimir Jabotinsky, *The Jewish State—Solution to the Jewish Problem* (1936), excerpted in *Political and Social Philosophy*, 132.

92 Albert Memmi, *Portrait of the Jew*, trans. Elisabeth Abbott (New York: Orion, 1962), 244–6.

93 Theodor Herzl, "The Jews as a Pioneer People," Spring 1899, Vienna, in *Zionist Writings*, vol. 2, 66.

94 The unity of oppressed peoples in a struggle against their oppressors was Arendt's preferred strategy for the European Jews, which was far easier for her to imagine, because she did not buy Herzl's definition of a nation and so could contemplate both the Jews' participation in a larger political struggle for freedom and their continued existence as Jews in a multi-ethnic society that such a struggle might bring about.

95 Memmi, *Liberation of the Jew*, 283.

96 Joseph B. Schechtman, *The Life and Times of Vladimir Jabotinsky*, vol. 1, *Rebel and Statesman: The Early Years* (New York: Eshel Books, 1986, 1956), 47. Schechtman recounts these words from Jabotinsky's first public speech at 17 years of age.

97 Theodor Herzl, "The Family Affliction," *The American Hebrew*, January 13, 1899, in *Zionist Writings*, vol. 2, 45.

98 Jabotinsky, *Jewish War Front*, 115.

99 Theodor Herzl, "Zionism," Fall 1899, in *Zionist Writings*, vol. 2, 111.

100 Herzl, *Jewish State*, 129.

101 Herzl, "For a Jewish State," in *Zionist Writings*, vol. 1, 37.

102 Herzl, *Jewish State*, 112.

103 Ibid., 138.

104 Herzl, *Diaries of Theodor Herzl*, June 7, 1895 entry, 37.

105 This select few would investigate the new national territory, orchestrate immigration to it, raise the requisite funds, and develop new political

institutions. Herzl hoped that a similarly select few would serve in the new government as a sovereign "counterpoise" to the power of the people.

106 Herzl, *Jewish State*, 157, 92, 153–4.

107 Valdimir Jabotinsky, "Parliament," *Haaretz*, May 21, 1925, excerpted in *Political and Social Philosophy*, 102.

108 Vladimir Jabotinsky, "Vos Erger Alts Besser," *De Tribune*, 25 April, 1926, excerpted in ibid., 109. While Jabotinsky is thus well aware of the anti-colonial thrust of Arab resistance to Zionism, he as well as Schechtman emphatically refer to popular Arab violence against the increase of Jewish immigration to Palestine in the 1920s and early 1930s as "pogroms," a word that, while it strictly speaking connotes "riots," conveys the message that the animating passion of such riots was anti-Semitism, and not, in this instance, anti-colonialism. For example, see Schechtman, *Vladimir Jabotinsky*, vol. 1, 362, 379, 385. Khalidi describes the same violence instead as a response to the growing landlessness and unemployment among Palestinian peasants as a result of Zionist land acquisitions and Jewish-only labor policies. Khalidi, *Iron Cage*, 86.

109 Vladimir Jabotinsky, "On the Sanctity of the Police," *Hazit Haam*, 8 January, 1934, excerpted in *Political and Social Philosophy*, 43.

110 Vladimir Jabotinsky, "Address before British Members of Parliament," 13 July, 1937, *Speeches, 1927–1940*, excerpted in ibid., 103.

111 Vladimir Jabotinsky, "Foolish Vanity," *Hayarden*, February 12, 1938, excerpted in ibid., 106.

112 Vladimir Jabotinsky, "The Iron Wall," *The Jewish Herald*, November 6, 1937, excerpted in ibid., 105.

113 Vladimir Jabotinsky, "Address to the Eretz-Israel Council, 1919, *Speeches 1905–1926*, excerpted in ibid., 94.

114 Vladimir Jabotinsky, "A Lecture on Israeli History," *Umah ve-Havrah*, 1959, quoted in Kaplan *The Jewish Radical Right*, 49. Jabotinsky uses the same "no connecting bridge" and "Iron Wall" metaphors to describe other un-crossable chasms, including one between British anti-Semitic officials and armed Zionists in Palestine, and even between his own hard line towards the British and Arabs, and the World Zionist Organization's lenient one. See Schechtman, *Vladimir Jabotinsky*, vol. 1, 380, 436.

115 Jabotinsky, "The Ideology of the Betar," *From the Pen of Jabotinsky*, 37.

116 Vladimir Jabotinsky, "Ethics of the Iron Wall," *Rasswiyet*, 1923, excerpted in *Political and Social Philosophy*, 105.

117 Jabotinsky, *The Jewish War Front*, 213–20.

118 Vladimir Jabotinsky, Recording of a speech to the Jewish population in Palestine, 1937, excerpted in *Political and Social Philosophy*, 101.

119 Jabotinsky, "On State and Social Problems," *From the Pen of Jabotinsky*, 60–1.

120 This is according to Mordechai Sarig, who says that Jabotinsky put these words in the mouth of an unknown spokesman for the Jewish nation. "Editor's Note," in *Political and Social Philosophy*, xxv–xxvi.

Conclusions and Extrapolations

1 I offer an Arendtian reading of these efforts in Joan Cocks, "Is the Right to Sovereignty a Human Right? The Idea of Sovereign Freedom and the Jewish State," in *Silencing Human Rights: Critical Engagements with a Contested Project*, ed. Gurminder K. Bhambra and Robbie Shilliam (Houndmills, England: Palgrave Macmillan, 2009), 105–23.

2 Other villages resisting Israeli Occupation in the same way include Budrus, Nabi Saleh, Biddu, Ni'lin, and Al Ma'asara. See Ben Ehrenreich, "The Resisters," *New York Times Sunday Magazine*, March 17, 2013, 24–31 and 50–1.

3 See especially James C. Scott, *Seeing like a State: How Certain Schemes to Improve the Human Condition Have Failed* (New Haven, CT: Yale University Press, 1998) and *The Art of Not Being Governed: An Anarchist History of Upland Southeast Asia* (New Haven, CT: Yale University Press, 2009).

4 Wendy Brown, *Walled States, Waning Sovereignty* (New York: Zone Books, 2010), 64–5.

5 For a like-minded but far more extended argument against liberal ideas of Progress, see Uday Singh Mehta, *Liberalism and Empire* (Chicago: University of Chicago Press, 1999).

6 Karl Marx, *Capital*, vol. 1, ed. Frederick Engels, trans. Samuel Moore and Edward Aveling (New York: International Publishers, 1967 [1867]), 713–74.

7   Rosa Luxemburg, *The Accumulation of Capital*, trans. Agnes
     Schwarzschild (London: Routledge and Kegan Paul, 1963 [1913]),
     Chapters XXVI–XXXII. However mistaken she might have been about
     the necessity of non-capitalist environments for profit-making, and
     however misplaced her faith in the proletarian revolution as an almost
     unstoppable "locomotive of history," Luxemburg was keenly sensitive to
     the virtues of pre-capitalist, non-capitalist, and early capitalist historical
     moments.

8   See, for example, Raymond Williams, *The Country and the City*
     (Oxford: Oxford University Press, 1973), and E. P. Thompson, "Time,
     Work-Discipline, and Industrial Capitalism," *Past and Present*, no. 38:
     56–97 and "The Moral Economy of the English Crowd in the Eighteenth
     Century," *Past and Present*, no. 50: 76–136.

9   David Harvey, *The New Imperialism* (Oxford University Press, 2005,
     2003), Chapter 4.

10   Yuri Slezkine, *The Jewish Century* (Princeton, NJ: Princeton University
     Press, 2004), 367.

11   Not that theoretical nation-deconstructions and recommendations
     for non-national or international laws and norms can't stimulate the
     political imagination. For example, see Jacqueline Stevens, *States without
     Nations: Citizenship for Mortals* (New York: Columbia University, 2010)
     and, in a different vein, Seyla Benhabib, *The Rights of Others: Aliens,
     Residents, and Citizens* (Cambridge: Cambridge University Press, 2007,
     2004).

12   California's recent to attempt to invite resident aliens to serve on jury
     panels promised to be, if only for the moment before it was stymied,
     another step forward for Mercurians in that state.

13   Patchen Markell, *Bound by Recognition* (Princeton, NJ: Princeton
     University Press, 2003), 22.

14   Pope Francis, as quoted in James Carroll, "Who am I to Judge? A radical
     Pope's first year," *New Yorker*, December 23 and 30, 2013, 88.

Bibliography

Abu El-Haj, Nadia. *Facts on the Ground: Archaeological Practice and Territorial Self-Fashioning in Israeli Society*. Chicago: University of Chicago Press, 2001.

Agamben, Giorgio. *Homo Sacer: Sovereign Power and Bare Life*. Translated by Daniel Heller-Roazen. Stanford, CA: Stanford University Press, 1998.

Agnew, John. *Globalization and Sovereignty*. Lanham, MD: Rowman & Littlefield, 2009.

Alfred, Taiaiake. *Peace, Power, Righteousness: An Indigenous Manifesto*. Don Mills, ON: Oxford University Press, 1999.

Arendt, Hannah. *The Jew as Pariah: Jewish Identity and Politics in the Modern Age*. Edited by Ron H. Feldman. New York: Grove Press, 1978.

— "The Jewish State: Fifty Years After: *Where Have Herzl's Politics Led?* (May 1946). In Arendt, *The Jew as Pariah*, 164–77.

—*Men in Dark Times*. New York: Harcourt Brace Jovanovich, 1968 (1955).

—*On Revolution*. New York: Penguin Classics, 2006 (1963).

—*The Origins of Totalitarianism*. New York: Harcourt Brace, 1973 (1951).

— "What is Freedom?" in Hannah Arendt, *Between Past and Future: Eight Exercises in Political Thought*. New York: Penguin, 2006 (1961).

— "Zionism Reconsidered" (October 1944). In Arendt, *The Jew as Pariah*, 131–63.

Augustine. *The Political Writings of St. Augustine*. Edited by Henry Paolucci. South Bend, IN: Regnery Gateway, 1962.

Balibar, Etienne. *We, the People of Europe? Reflections on Transnational Citizenship*. Translated by James Swenson. Princeton, NJ: Princeton University Press, 2004.

Banfield, Edward C. "Was the Founding an Accident?" In Kesler, *Saving the Revolution*, 265–75. New York: Free Press, 1987.

Benhabib, Seyla. *The Rights of Others: Aliens, Residents, and Citizens*. Cambridge: Cambridge University Press, 2007, 2004.

Benvenisti, Meron. *Sacred Landscape: The Buried History of the Holy Land since 1948*. Translated by Maxine Kaufman-Lacusta. Berkeley: University of California Press, 2000.

Blackbourn, David. *The Conquest of Nature: Water, Landscape, and the Making of Modern Germany*. New York: W. W. Norton, 2006.

Bodin, Jean. *On Sovereignty: Four chapters from "The Six Books of the Commonwealth."* Edited and translated by Julian H. Franklin. Cambridge: Cambridge University Press, 2006, 1992 (1576).

Bollier, David. *Silent Theft: The Private Plunder of our Common Wealth.* New York: Routledge, 2003.

Brown, Wendy. *Walled States, Waning Sovereignty.* New York: Zone Books, 2010.

Bruyneel, Kevin. *The Third Space of Sovereignty: The Postcolonial Politics of U.S.—Indigenous Relations.* Minneapolis: University of Minnesota, 2007.

Burke, Edmund. *Reflections on the Revolution in France.* In *Reflections on the Revolution in France and The Rights of Man.* New York: Anchor Books, 1973 (1790).

Butler, Judith. *Precarious Life: The Powers of Mourning and Violence.* London: Verso, 2006, 2004.

Carroll, James. "Who am I to Judge? A radical Pope's first year." *New Yorker,* December 23 and 30, 2013, 80–91.

Cheyfitz, Eric. *The Poetics of Imperialism: Translation and Colonialism from "The Tempest" to "Tarzan."* New York: Oxford University Press, 1991.

Clastres, Pierre. *Society Against the State: The Leader as Servant and the Humane Uses of Power Among the Indians of the Americas.* Translated by Robert Hurley. New York: Urizen Books, 1977, 1974.

Cocks, Joan. "Is the Right to Sovereignty a Human Right? The Idea of Sovereign Freedom and the Jewish State." In *Silencing Human Rights: Critical Engagements with a Contested Project.* Edited by Gurminder K. Bhambra and Robbie Shilliam. Houndmills, England: Palgrave Macmillan, 2009, 105–23.

Cohen, G. A. "History, Ethics, and Marxism." In *Canadian Political Philosophy: Contemporary Reflections.* Edited by Ronald Beiner and Wayne Norman. Oxford: Oxford University Press, 2001, 107–17.

Collier, David, Fernando Daniel Hidalgo and Andra Olivia Maciuceanu. "Essentially Contested Concepts: Debates and Applications." *Journal of Political Ideologies* 11, no. 3 (October 2006): 211–46.

Connolly, William E. *Pluralism.* Durham, NC: Duke University Press, 2005.

—*The Terms of Political Discourse.* Lexington, MA: D. C. Heath, 1974.

Cronon, William. *Changes in the Land: Indians, Colonists, and the Ecology of New England.* New York: Hill and Wang, 1983.

Delaune, Timothy A. "Democratizing the Criminal: Jury Nullification as Exercise of Sovereign Discretion over the Friend-Enemy Distinction." PhD diss. University of Massachusetts, Amherst, 2013.

Deloria Jr., Vine, and Raymond J. DeMallie, eds. *Documents of American Indian Diplomacy: Treaties, Agreements, and Conventions, 1775–1979.* Norman: University of Oklahoma Press, 1999.

Derrida, Jacques. "Force of Law: The 'Mystical Foundation of Authority.'" In Jacques Derrida, *Acts of Religion*, edited by Gil Anidjar, 228–98. New York: Routledge, 2002.

Dostoyevsky, Fyodor. *Crime and Punishment.* Translated by Richard Pevear and Larissa Volokhonsky. New York: Vintage, 1993 (1867).

Edmonds, R. David. *Tecumseh and the Quest for Indian Leadership.* 2nd ed. New York: Pearson Longman, 2007.

Elkins, Stanley, and Eric McKitrick. *The Age of Federalism: The Early American Republic, 1788–1800.* Oxford: Oxford University Press, 1993.

Fanon, Frantz. *The Wretched of the Earth.* Translated by Constance Farrington. New York: Grove Weidenfeld, 1991 (1963).

Freud, Sigmund. *The Future of an Illusion.* In *The Freud Reader.* Edited by Peter Gay. New York: W. W. Norton, 1989 (1927).

Gallie, W. B. "Essentially Contested Concepts." *Proceedings of the Aristotelian Society* 56 (1955–6): 167–98.

Gordon, Neve. *Israel's Occupation.* Berkeley: University of California Press, 2008.

Gorny, Yosef. *From Binational Society to Jewish State: Federal Concepts in Zionist Political Thought, 1920–1990, and the Jewish People.* Leiden, The Netherlands: Brill, 2006.

Grande, Sandy. *Red Pedagogy: Native American Social and Political Thought.* Lanham, MD: Rowman & Littlefield, 2004.

Halper, Jeff. *An Israeli in Palestine: Resisting Dispossession, Redeeming Israel.* London: Pluto Press, 2010 (2008).

Hardt, Michael, and Antonio Negri. *Empire.* Cambridge, MA: Harvard University Press, 2000.

Harvey, David. *The New Imperialism.* Oxford University Press, 2005, 2003.

Hertzberg, Arthur, ed. *The Zionist Idea.* New York: Atheneum Macmillan, 1969, 1959.

Herzl, Theodor. *Altneuland.* Translated by Paula Arnold. Haifa: Haifa Publishing, 1960 (1902).

—*The Diaries of Theodor Herzl.* Edited and translated by Marvin Lowenthal. New York: Dial Press, 1956.

—*The Jewish State: An Attempt at a Modern Solution of the Jewish Question*. New York: American Zionist Emergency Council, 1946 (1896).

—*Zionist Writings: Essays and Addresses*. Vol. 1, *January 1896—June 1898*. Translated by Harry Zohn. New York: The Herzl Press, 1973.

—*Zionist Writings: Essays and Addresses*. Vol. 2, *August, 1898—May, 1904*. Translated by Harry Zohn. New York: Herzl Press, 1973.

Hobbes, Thomas. *Leviathan*. Edited by Richard Tuck. Cambridge: Cambridge University Press, 2005, 1996 (1651).

Honig, Bonnie. *Emergency Politics: Paradox, Law, Democracy*. Princeton, NJ: Princeton University Press, 2011, 2009.

—"Toward an Agonistic Feminism: Hannah Arendt and the Politics of Identity." In *Feminist Interpretations of Hannah Arendt*, edited by Bonnie Honig, 135–66. University Park: Pennsylvania State University Press, 1995.

Howes, Dustin. *Toward a Credible Pacifism*. Albany: State University of New York Press, 2009.

Hsueh, Vicki. *Hybrid Constitutions: Challenging Legacies of Law, Privilege, and Culture in Colonial America*. Durham, NC: Duke University Press, 2010.

Hurewitz, J. C. *The Struggle for Palestine*. New York: W. W. Norton, 1950.

Jabotinsky, Vladimir. *From the Pen of Jabotinsky*. Capetown, South Africa: Unie-Volkspers BPK, 1941.

—"The Ideology of the Betar." In Jabotinsky, *From the Pen of Jabotinsky*, 35–59.

—*The Jewish War Front*. London: George Allen & Unwin, 1940.

—*The Political and Social Philosophy of Ze'ev Jabotinsky: Selected Writings*. Edited by Mordechai Sarig. Translated by Shimshon Feder. London: Vallentine Mitchell, 1999.

—"On State and Social Problems." In Jabotinsky, *From the Pen of Jabotinsky*, 60–77.

—*The Story of the Jewish Legion*. Edited and translated by Samuel Katz. New York: Bernard Ackerman, 1945.

Jaffa, Harry V. *How to Think about the American Revolution*. Durham: University of North Carolina Press, 1978.

Jones, Dorothy V. *License for Empire: Colonialism by Treaty in Early America*. Chicago: University of Chicago Press, 1982.

Jung, Courtney. *The Moral Force of Indigenous Politics: Critical Liberalism and the Zapatistas*. Cambridge: Cambridge University Press, 2008.

Kafka, Franz. *The Trial*. Translated by Willa Muir and Edwin Muir. New York: Modern Library, 1956 (1925).

Kaplan, Eran. *The Jewish Radical Right: Revisionist Zionism and its Ideological Legacy*. Madison, WI: University of Wisconsin Press, 2005.

Kappler, Charles J., ed. *Indian Affairs: Laws and Treaties*. Vol. 2, *Treaties*. Washington, DC: Government Printing Office, 1904.

Kesler, Charles R., ed. *Saving the Revolution: The Federalist Papers and the American Founding*. New York: Free Press, 1987.

Khalidi, Rashid. *The Iron Cage: The Story of the Palestinian Struggle for Statehood*. Boston: Beacon Press, 2006.

Kowtko, Stacy. *Nature and the Environment in Pre-Columbian American Life*. Westport, CT: Greenwood Press, 2006.

Krouse, Sharon. "Freedom Beyond Sovereignty." politicalscience.stanford.edu/ Workshops/Political Theory Workshop/Sharon Krouse (March 9, 2012).

Laqueur, Walter. *A History of Zionism*. New York: Schocken Books, 1976 (1972).

Lloyd, David. "Settler Colonialism and the State of Exception: The Example of Palestine/Israel." In "Past is Present": 59–80.

Lockman, Zachary. "Land, Labor and the Logic of Zionism: A Critical Engagement with Gershon Shafir." In "Past is Present": 9–38.

Lubasz, Heinz. *The Development of the Modern State*. New York: Macmillan, 1964.

Lustick, Ian. *Arabs in the Jewish State: Israel's Control of a National Minority*. Austin: University of Texas, 1980.

Luxemburg, Rosa. *The Accumulation of Capital*. Translated by Agnes Schwarzschild. London: Routledge and Kegan Paul, 1963 (1913).

Machiavelli, Niccolò. *The Discourses*. New York: Penguin, 1970, 1998 (1531).

—*The Prince*. Edited by Quentin Skinner and Russell Price. Cambridge: Cambridge University Press, 1988 (1532).

Madison, James, Alexander Hamilton, and John Jay. *The Federalist Papers*. Edited by Isaac Kramnick. London: Penguin Classics, 1987 (1788).

Mann, Michael. *The Dark Side of Democracy: Explaining Ethnic Cleansing*. Cambridge: Cambridge University Press, 2009, 2005.

Mantena, Karuna. "Another Realism: The Politics of Gandhian Nonviolence." *The American Political Science Review* 106, no. 2 (May 2012): 455–70.

Markell, Patchen. *Bound by Recognition*. Princeton, NJ: Princeton University Press, 2003.

—"The Rule of the People: Arendt, *Archê*, and Democracy." *American Political Science Review* 100, no. 1 (February 2006): 1–14.

Marx, Karl. *Capital*. Vol. 1. Edited by Frederick Engels. Translated by Samuel Moore and Edward Aveling. New York: International Publishers, 1967 (1867).

Mazower, Mark. *Salonica, City of Ghosts: Christians, Muslims and Jews 1430–1950*. New York: Alfred A. Knopf, 2005.

Mehta, Uday Singh. *Liberalism and Empire*. Chicago: University of Chicago Press, 1999.

Memmi, Albert. *Decolonization and the Decolonized*. Translated by Robert Bononno. Minneapolis: University of Minnesota Press, 2006, 2004.

—*Jews and Arabs*. Translated by Eleanor Levieux. Chicago: J. Philip O'Hara, 1975.

—*The Liberation of the Jew*. Translated by Judy Hyun. New York: Viking, 1973, 1966.

—*Portrait of the Jew*. Translated by Elisabeth Abbott. New York: Orion, 1962.

Mill, J. S. "On Liberty." In *John Stuart Mill: Three Essays*. Edited by Richard Wollheim. Oxford: Oxford University Press, 1975 (1857).

Morgan, Edmund. *Inventing the People: The Rise of Popular Sovereignty in England and America*. New York: W. W. Norton, 1988.

Morris, Bennie. *Righteous Victims: A History of the Zionist–Arab Conflict, 1881–1999*. New York: Alfred A. Knopf, 1999.

Nietzsche, Friedrich. *On the Genealogy of Morals*. Translated by Walter Kaufmann and R. J. Hollingdale. New York: Vintage Books, 1969 (1887).

Onuf, Nicholas Greenwood. "Sovereignty: Outline of a Conceptual History." *Alternatives* 16 (1991): 425–46.

"Past is Present: Settler Colonialism in Palestine." Special issue, *Settler Colonial Studies* 2, no. 1 (2012).

Patterson, Orlando. *Freedom*. Vol. 1, *Freedom in the Making of Western Culture*. New York: Basic Books, 1991.

Philpott, Daniel. *Revolutions in Sovereignty: How Ideas Shaped Modern International Relations*. Princeton, NJ: Princeton University Press, 2001.

Pocock, J. G. A. *The Machiavellian Moment: Florentine Political Thought and the Atlantic Republican Tradition*. Princeton, NJ: Princeton University Press, 1975.

Prucha, Francis Paul. *American Indian Treaties: The History of a Political Anomaly*. Berkeley: University of California Press, 1994.

Remnick, David. "The Party Faithful." *New Yorker*, January 21, 2013, 38–49.

Robertson, Ritchie, and Edward Timms, eds. *Theodor Herzl and the Origins of Zionism*. Edinburgh: Edinburgh University Press, 1997.

Rodinson, Maxime. *Cult, Ghetto, and State: The Persistence of the Jewish Question*. London: Al Saqi Books, 1983.

Rohl, John C. G. "Herzl and Kaiser Wilhelm II: A German Protectorate in Palestine?" In Robertson and Timms, *Theodor Herzl and the Origins of Zionism*, 27–38.

Rousseau, Jean-Jacques. *The Social Contract or Principles of Political Right*. Translated by Maurice Cranston. London: Penguin Classics, 1968 (1762).

Sassen, Saskia. *Losing Control? Sovereignty in an Age of Globalization*. New York: Columbia University Press, 1996.

Sayre, Gordon M. *The Indian Chief as Tragic Hero: Native Resistance and the Literatures of America, from Moctezuma to Tecumseh*. Chapel Hill: University of North Carolina Press, 2005.

Scarry, Elaine. *The Body in Pain*. Oxford: Oxford University Press, 1985.

Schechtman, Joseph B. *The Life and Times of Vladimir Jabotinsky*. Vol. 1, *Rebel and Statesman: The Early Years*. New York: Eshel Books, 1986, 1956.

—*The Life and Times of Jabotinsky*. Vol. 2, *Fighter and Prophet: The Last Years*. Silver Springs, MD: Eshel Books, 1986, 1961.

Schmitt, Carl. *Political Theology: Four Chapters on the Concept of Sovereignty*. Translated by George Schwab. Chicago: University of Chicago, 2005 (1922).

Scott, James C. *The Art of Not Being Governed: An Anarchist History of Upland Southeast Asia*. New Haven, CT: Yale University Press, 2009.

—*Seeing like a State: How Certain Schemes to Improve the Human Condition Have Failed*. New Haven, CT: Yale University Press, 1998.

Segev, Tom. *1949: The First Israelis*. New York: Henry Holt, 1998, 1986.

Shahak, Israel, and Norton Mezvinsky. *Jewish Fundamentalism in Israel*. New edn. London: Pluto Press, 2004.

Shavit, Yaacov. *Jabotinsky and the Revisionist Movement 1925–1948*. London: Frank Cass, 1988.

Skinner, Quentin. *Liberty before Liberalism*. Cambridge: Cambridge University Press, 1998.

Slezkine, Yuri. *The Jewish Century*. Princeton, NJ: Princeton University Press, 2004.

Standing, Guy. *The Precariat: The New Dangerous Class*. London: Bloomsbury Academic, 2011.

Stanislawski, Michael. *Zionism and the Fin de Siècle: Cosmopolitanism and*

Nationalism from Nordau to Jabotinsky. Berkeley: University of California Press, 2001.

Stannard, David E. *American Holocaust: The Conquest of the New World.* Oxford: Oxford University Press, 1992.

Stevens, Jacqueline. *States without Nations: Citizenship for Mortals.* New York: Columbia University, 2010.

Strauss, Leo. *Natural Right and History.* Chicago: University of Chicago Press, 1965, 1950.

Sugden, John. *Tecumseh: A Life.* New York: Henry Holt, 1998.

Teveth, Shabtai. *Ben-Gurion and the Palestinian Arabs: From Peace to War.* Oxford: Oxford University Press, 1985.

Thompson, E. P. "The Moral Economy of the English Crowd in the Eighteenth Century." *Past and Present*, no. 50: 76–136.

—"Time, Work-Discipline, and Industrial Capitalism." *Past and Present*, no. 38: 56–97.

Timms, Edward. "Ambassador Herzl and the Blueprint for a Modern State." In Robertson and Timms, *Theodor Herzl and the Origins of Zionism*, 12–26.

Tully, James. *Public Philosophy in a New Key.* Vol. 1, *Democracy and Civic Freedom.* Cambridge: Cambridge University Press, 2008.

Turner, Dale. *This is Not a Peace Pipe: Towards a Critical Indigenous Philosophy.* Toronto: University of Toronto Press, 2006.

Vital, David. *The Origins of Zionism.* Oxford: Clarendon Press, 1980, 1975.

Weber, Max. "Politics as a Vocation." In *From Max Weber: Essays in Sociology*, edited and translated by H. H. Gerth and C. Wright Mills, 77–128. New York: Oxford University Press, 1958, 1946 (1919).

Weizman, Eyal. *Hollow Land: Israel's Architecture of Occupation.* London: Verso, 2007.

Wildenthal, Bryan H. *Native American Sovereignty on Trial: A Handbook with Cases, Laws, and Documents.* Santa Barbara, CA: ABC-CLIO, 2003.

Wilder, Gary. "Irreconcilable Differences: A Conversation with Albert Memmi." *Transition*, Issue 71 (1996): 158–77.

Wilkins, David E. *American Indian Sovereignty and the U.S. Supreme Court: The Masking of Justice.* Austin: University of Texas Press, 1997.

Wilkins, David E., and K. Tsianina Lomawaima. *Uneven Ground: American Indian Sovereignty and Federal Law.* Norman: University of Oklahoma Press, 2001.

Williams, Raymond. *The Country and the City.* Oxford: Oxford University Press, 1973.

—*Marxism and Literature.* Oxford: Oxford University Press, 1977.

Wood, Gordon S. *The Radicalism of the American Revolution.* New York: Alfred A. Knopf, 1991.

Zertal, Idith. "From the People's Hall to the Wailing Wall: A Study in Memory, Fear, and War." *Representations* 69 (Winter 2000): 96–126.

Index

Jabotinsky, Vladimir and 120–2
non-sovereignty and 126–8
protests and 127–8
refugees and 97
settlement and 99
sovereign freedom and 123–4
paradoxes 28
people, the 53, 55
and the mob 113
philosophical liberals 20–1
Philpott, Daniel 21
political authority 48–51, 56
political concepts 1–2, 12–13
political discourse 11–18
political science 13–14, 19
political theory 2, 6, 8, 19, 138
"Politics as a Vocation" (1946)
(Weber) 49
popular sovereign power 3, 23–4,
63–4, 78, 97, 113–14, 144n. 16
Portrait of the Jew, The (1962)
(Memmi) 109
post-modernism 1
poststructuralism 21–2
Prince, the 31–2
Prince, The (1532) (Machiavelli) 52–3
progress 1, 128–31, 135

race 84, 92–6, 102–3 *see also*
American Indians;
anti–Semitism
*Radicalism of the American
Revolution, The* (1991)
(Wood) 64
refugees, Palestinian 95, 97
Rome, founding of 48
Rousseau, Jean-Jacques 39, 44, 113
Social Contract, The (1762) 37–8
Russian communism and
nationalism 133–4
Rwandan genocide 23

Said, Edward 16–17
Sassen, Saskia 26

Scott, James C. 130
secularization 40–1
self, the 44, 105
self-rule 16, 77–8
settler colonial projects 5, 51–2, 101,
119–20 *see also* American
Indians; indigenous peoples
Six-Day War 97
Skinner, Quentin 15–16
Slezkine, Yuri: *Jewish Century, The*
(2004) 132–4
Social Contract, The (1762)
(Rousseau) 37–8
social extermination 81
social types 132–6
Apollonian 132–4, 136
Mercurian 132–6
sovereign freedom 4, 5, 9–10, 105,
122–3 *see also* freedom;
natural freedom
Arendt, Hannah and 40–4
beginning and perpetuating 43
Bodin, Jean and 31
Burke, Edmund and 39–40
consequences of 40
domination and 43–5
Europe and 35–6
finitude and 136–7
General Will and 37–8
indigenous peoples and 76
Israel and 103–4, 106, 110–4,
118–24
popular 38–40
Rousseau, Jean-Jacques and 36–7,
39
secularization and 40–1
self, and the 44–5
versus sovereign power 4
sovereign individual, the 4, 20
sovereign power 2–4, 18–27,
78, 104–5 *see also*
counter–sovereignty
appeal of 26–30
Israel and 103–4, 110–4, 118–22